From Dental Floss To Guitar Strings

Successful Grassroots Product Launches

BookLocker

Saint Petersburg, Florida

Published by BookLocker.com, Inc., St. Petersburg, Florida.

Printed on acid-free paper.

Paperback ISBN: 978-1-64719-706-3
Hardcover ISBN: 978-1-64719-707-0
Ebook ISBN: 978-1-64719-708-7

BookLocker.com, Inc.
2021

Bucktown Grand Slam
Buchanan, Michigan

Dedicated to Pamela, my wife and best friend.
GLIDE® Floss and ELIXIR® Strings would not exist but for
Pam's support and encouragement.

A special thank you to my teammates who worked endless
hours in making GLIDE Floss and ELIXIR Strings
successful. I also want to thank my friend, David Johns, for
his ongoing encouragement and reviews of draft manuscripts.

This book is in memory of Ritchie Snyder,
my coach and mentor.

www.bucktowngrandslam.com

John@bucktowngrandslam.com

Table of Contents

Introduction

You have an idea for a new product.

Great! Every success story begins with an idea.

Grassroots product launches work.

What should you do now?

I suggest you develop and manufacture a product from your idea that the customer values and execute an inspired grassroots product launch plan. Grassroots is code for (1) not having a massive budget to hire dozens of people or (2) launching your new product with a Super Bowl ad. Grassroots marketing is educating select people about your product's benefits to create buzz and sustainable customer demand. Grassroots marketing sounds easy, but it takes planning, persistence, and trust that you have solved the puzzle of your grassroots product launch.

I can help you.

Reading this book can help you and your team increase your chance of successfully launching a new product with a limited budget.

The consensus is that less than 20% of new products make money, which means at least 80% fail. An experienced gambler wins 45% of the time, and anyone can win 35% of the time by picking the favorite horse at the track. Considering these statistics, launching new products seems riskier than gambling, doesn't it? A professional gambler works hard to improve the winning percentage by studying the games, understanding the odds, and playing to a plan. You must think along the same lines to improve your odds of successfully launching a new product.

I have lived and breathed the development and successful launch of disruptive and high-value consumer products in a high-technology company. My goal in telling these stories is for you to learn from my firsthand experience and look at the product launch game from a new perspective.

Stop! Are you passionate?

Success requires a passion for your product and a commitment to action. You must also be lucky. But luck is often simply attitude and hard work. Do not let the scoundrels get you down; believe in yourself and your team members. If you begin a project with failure as an option, you will fail. It is confidence, not arrogance, to believe you will win. Finally, balance this passion with objectivity.

What is in this book?

Part 1 is a memoir and features my stories of leading successful consumer product launches featuring grassroots marketing.

The first story is the development and launch of GLIDE Floss, the top-selling dental floss. It is a "David and Goliath" story that begins and ends with the author's firing. GLIDE Floss demonstrates how a great idea with a brilliant grassroots marketing plan can disrupt a company and the market and result in commercial success.

The GLIDE Floss story may not make sense to many people who have worked for corporations. How did an engineer and manufacturing plant manager with no business experience lead a new and disruptive business launch? Lesson 5, Leadership and Teams, describes W. L. Gore & Associates, Inc., a great company that allows Associates maximum freedom to grow and learn. I am a beneficiary of Gore's unique culture and the inspirational leadership of Ritchie Snyder.

The next story is about ELIXIR Strings, the top-selling acoustic guitar string. ELIXIR Strings was a complex product to develop, and the odds of commercial success were low. ELIXIR Strings is the story of an exceptional team coming together to overcome significant product, pricing, and market obstacles. Grassroots marketing and a disciplined sales strategy won the day.

Part 2 is a fresh look at critical lessons learned in launching new products and how you can improve your chances of achieving grassroots success.

I discuss six lessons in launching new products that will improve your odds of business success. New products are a puzzle, but you must simultaneously work on multiple pieces of the puzzle for success. Unfortunately, many engineers focus solely on product specifications, and they are like the dog who catches the car it has been chasing with no idea what to do once the product works.

Launching new products is exciting, and you will build relationships with people that will last a lifetime. But launches are also challenging, nerve-wracking, and overwhelming. Big mistakes can be ruinous, but I encourage small mistakes to test and learn. No one remembers small mistakes. I will help you prioritize the many necessary actions for you to have fun and to triumph. There are no guarantees for success, but you can almost guarantee failure if you are not prepared.

Part 2 lessons include framing the product value statement, strategic planning, pricing, grassroots marketing and sales, leadership and teams, and financial planning.

Do you want to succeed?

Of course, you want to succeed, and success always beats failure. I know this from personal experience. Remember, a product is just an idea until you have profitable sales and loyal customers. It is not easy. If it were, anyone could do it. Believe in yourself and think "grassroots."

Thanks.

John S.

Bucktown Grand Slam

Buchanan, Michigan

Part 1:
A Memoir

I led the launch of two leading consumer products, GLIDE Floss and ELIXIR Strings.

Part 1 presents the story of the launch of these exceptional new products.

Story 1. GLIDE Floss

Do Not Get Fired

I begin this story with some good advice: Do not get fired from your job.

Many business experts advise people to "go to work each day willing to be fired for doing the right thing." How can you argue with this? Being fired from your life's work is not fun. It is deeply unsettling to you and your family. Being fired becomes a part of your brand, and folklore will replace reality to explain the firing reasons. As Mark Twain said, "A lie can travel halfway around the world while the truth is putting on its shoes." My advice is to go to work each day and do the right thing. If your company is not doing the right thing, refresh your resume and move to a better company or start your own company.

I have more advice. If you lose your job, plot a path forward as fast as possible. Moving on can be difficult, especially if the circumstances feel unfair. My bet is most people fired from a job are not saying, "I cannot believe it took this long for them to fire me." Life is not always fair. Deal with it quickly.

I am lucky. My wife, Pamela, helped me navigate my future after losing two jobs. She understands my strengths and weaknesses. Pam knows when to kick me in the butt or listen to my woes. Yes, the GLIDE Floss story begins and ends with me looking for work.

The Beginning – You Are Fired

On August 10, 1990, I worked at the Gore Polymer Products Plant as a manufacturing plant manager and engineer in Newark, Delaware. At two o'clock in the afternoon, I received a phone call, and company leadership directed me to drive to Gore's headquarters, a short drive from the manufacturing plant. On arrival, executives, with my boss, dismissed me from the Gore company. I was shocked by this pronouncement. I have never seen myself as a person who would get fired. I had no bad performance reviews, my responsibilities continued to grow, and I made things happen consistent with the Gore company culture. I thought I had a bright future in the Gore company.

You do not know how you will react when losing your job. I listened attentively. My crime was not being a good follower of my boss in designing and constructing a new polymer manufacturing plant. I was disruptive and not the right kind of disruptive.

My biggest surprise in this meeting was how calm I was. It was almost an out-of-body experience, and I was on the sidelines watching a train wreck. I asked leadership to respond to their firing decision. I was composed, my tone of voice was even, and I was crisp. I agreed that I had been vocal in challenging recent direction from my boss to add two additional bays to the new polymer plant for unspecified use. I did not intend to be disrespectful, and I was spending company money as if it were my own. I designed the plant to allow for future additions to meet ongoing business needs. From my perspective, the additional building investment was premature and inconsistent with my commitment to managing costs effectively.

Suddenly, the lead executive stood and told the group to leave his office. I walked to an adjacent office with a Gore executive and my boss. I asked, "Am I fired?" The leader looked at me and said, "I will find out." He left, and after a few minutes, returned with a final decision. Leadership fired me from the Polymer Products Team, but not the Gore company. A condition of continued employment was to remain in my current job for six months to complete the construction and startup of the new 200,000 sq. ft. manufacturing plant, including the two additional manufacturing bays. In parallel, I would look for a new job in Gore or (implied) leave the company.

So, what happened?

I focused on building a new polymer manufacturing capability in Gore with a small team of exceptional people for five years. I focused on engineering, manufacturing, quality, process, costs, hiring, training, and delivering quality polymers on time to internal customers. I worked closely with Tommy Wallace, a great leader at Gore, and we shared a vision of innovation and operational excellence. The more money we spent, the higher our product's cost became to our internal customers. The polymers startup was a great success, and manufacturing had outgrown our rented facility. The company would invest in a new state-of-the-art polymers research facility and a manufacturing plant called "Elk Mills 1 Plant." Tommy and I focused on manufacturing automation and operational efficiency initiatives. The plant was beautiful, and

9

we did our best to manage construction costs actively. Building a new facility from scratch was challenging and fun.

But the Gore company had two objectives in building a new facility. First, an efficient polymer manufacturing plant, and second, a global polymer research center of excellence. I focused on manufacturing and failed to embrace and understand the broader technology capability fully. I objected to what I considered to be excess investments in last-minute manufacturing plant space additions with no specified purpose.

I had learned the best course of action would have been to schedule time with my boss, discuss my concerns, and sell a future building expansion when we needed the space for a specific activity. Unfortunately, I did not have the judgment to pull this off, but the good news is that I have learned from this experience. Perhaps I deserved to be fired? I do not think so. Sometimes the best advice leadership can offer to people with differing opinions is "work it out." Or Gore leadership could have worked with me for six months to find a new job without positioning my situation as a termination. I am surprised I did not update my resume and search for a new job. There are many good companies in Delaware and southeast Pennsylvania. But I liked the Gore company and its unique culture, and I did not want to leave. Gore had allowed me to grow far beyond my engineering training to gain manufacturing experience and plant leadership responsibilities. I was in my final year of law school at the University of Maryland, and Gore reimbursed my tuition. Gore actively supported my Naval Reserve responsibilities and two-week active-duty requirement. All good reasons to stay with the Gore company.

Now the good news. Being fired from the Polymer Products Team was one of the luckiest days of my life. Who would have guessed? Fate is strange, and it turns out that leaving the Gore company would have been a missed opportunity to learn and grow.

A New Opportunity

Finding a new job in a company is not easy, especially if the word on the street is that you are disruptive and have been fired from your current commitments. I decided the best course of action was to focus my time and energy on the new manufacturing plant construction and not rush to find a new job. In hindsight, I should have been seeking new commitments since Day One of being fired from the Polymer Products Team.

Construction of the new polymers plant went well, and in late October, I began my job search by scheduling meetings with Gore divisional leaders.

At the time, there were four operating divisions in the company. These included Electrical, Fabrics, Industrial, and Medical. The Medical Division was in Flagstaff, Arizona, and I did not see this business as an opportunity due to distance, and I was unwilling to move west. My first interview to explore a new job was with the Electrical Business Division leader. The leader began our discussion with a difficult question. He asked me, "What do you want to do?" I have never known what I wanted to do. I explained that my objective was to use my skills to impact a business positively. I had proven engineering and manufacturing skills, and I was in my final year of law school. I was also interested in learning general management skills, marketing, sales, business development, acquisitions, and regulatory law. I like variety and enjoy a learning environment. The leader was not impressed with my answer.

I asked the leader what gaps or challenges were limiting his business success? Without hesitation, he stated that there were no gaps in his business. Zero. You know what this means—I would not be working in the Electrical Division. His parting advice to me was that I take time and figure out my career objectives. I had a similar lack of success with the Fabrics Division leadership. I was surprised. They were customers for our polymers, and I thought the leaders would have appreciated my success in delivering quality products and managing costs. The interviews were friendly, but the Fabrics Division leadership "had no hiring needs that fit my experience." I reached out to an Industrial Sector leader. He said "no" to my query in a telephone call.

I now understood it was time to update my resume and begin an external job search.

My last meeting with Gore divisional leadership was with Ritchie Snyder. Ritchie was a leader in the Industrial business. I knew Ritchie but had never worked closely with him. Ritchie was a Gore family member and married to Betty, Bill and Vieve Gore's daughter, and Betty was on the Gore company Board of Directors.

I was not optimistic about my prospects.

Ritchie began our interview with one question, "When can you start?" And I replied, "The first working day of the new year." Ritchie suggested we would figure out what I would do after I joined his team. My interview was less than ten minutes. I had a job but no idea what it would be.

Ritchie lived and breathed the Gore company culture, and he is the best leader I have met in my life. I do not know why Ritchie hired me that day. Perhaps he was influenced by others to give me a chance. Regardless, his impact on my life has been extraordinary. I always ask myself what Ritchie would do when confronted with a challenging situation.

I began working for Ritchie on January 2, 1991. The plant was bustling with people returning to work from the holiday, and I met Ritchie first thing. He was genuinely excited to have me as a member of his team, and he made me feel welcome. Ritchie had decided on my job. I would start up a new business. Ritchie concluded that this was the best way to understand how his business operates and learn new skills. He had no concerns that I had minimal business skills and had never worked as a general manager or led a business startup. Ritchie would be my coach.

Ritchie had a chalkboard in his office that listed ten new business ideas that came up from time to time. One of the chalkboard businesses was dental floss made from Gore expanded PTFE fiber. Ritchie had investigated dental floss opportunities twenty years earlier and made business development calls to companies that were leaders in selling dental floss products. He joked that he received two orders after pitching the idea to a leading dental products company. Unfortunately, the orders were "Get out and stay out."

Gore had a short-term dental floss victory in the late 1980s when an oral health care company offered a dental floss product with Gore fiber without success. First, it was just an okay product. My memory is the denier was 800 or 900 versus 1150 denier used in GLIDE Floss. Denier is the weight in grams of 9,000 meters of fiber. For fiber buffs, denier is sometimes confused with DTEX, the weight in grams of 10,000 meters of fiber. The lower the denier material, the thinner the fiber. Pricing of the fiber is by the pound, so selecting a lower denier fiber offers more yards than a higher denier and lower material cost in the retail product. In short, they used too thin a fiber to lower costs and increase margins. Second, a new product requires a crisp marketing and sales strategy. The floss product was a relatively small addition to a broad range of oral health care products and packaged in a conventional private label floss dispenser. The sales pitch seems to have been, "Oh…and we have dental floss, too." An okay product in a lousy package, a lack of passion, and a weak sales pitch did not lead to success. Go figure.

Now back to my story. I liked the idea of leading a dental floss business startup. I flossed every day since I was eighteen. My sister, Priscilla Weaver, is an accomplished dental hygienist and became a free consultant for me.

But there is one challenge: I do not like or use GLIDE Floss. I prefer the cheap private label nylon dental floss that snaps into your gums and shreds. No pain, no gain. I took a fiber sample home and asked my wife, Pamela, to give it a try. She loved the floss from her first use, and I knew we were on to something. Pamela has a beautiful smile and tight contacts. Conventional nylon dental floss snaps into her gums, shreds and is uncomfortable for her to use. GLIDE Floss slides easily between teeth without shredding.

Ritchie gave me three months to build a business plan. I had not written a product business plan before, and I was excited about this new opportunity. Life takes an exciting twist.

The First Ninety Days

The first ninety days of any new project are overwhelming. There is just too much to do and not enough hours in the day. You survive by prioritizing activities to accomplish essential tasks. Every product or business is different. There are tools to help focus, but there are no templates that guarantee success. Not having consumer product experience contributed to a successful launch because I had no rules and was open to listening and learning. I am most creative when I do not know what I am doing. I repeat this observation in Part 2 of this book.

Gore's expected dental floss business model was to sell fiber to a leading consumer products company that would manufacture and sell a finished dental floss package in retail stores. The sale of Gore fiber as a dental floss best-case scenario is to be a component brand (e.g., COMPANY dental floss featuring GLIDE Fiber). I immediately reached out to companies that could benefit from selling premium dental floss. The response to a Gore fiber dental floss and fiber pricing was the same as in 1971. No interest. It is curious that every company immediately assumed a 15% maximum pricing premium, and margins were unacceptable. These are the experts.

Within a month, I had completed my research on the floss market and met with the leading players. I concluded that the only path for project success was for Gore to sell a branded consumer dental floss product to retail distribution and dental professionals. This idea seems reasonable today, but this was a radical idea at the time. Gore had no experience in selling a product in drugstores, grocery stores, or mass merchants. Furthermore, I had never launched a business or built a grassroots marketing plan.

I reviewed my thoughts with Ritchie, and he encouraged me to build a business plan for a Gore-branded product. I doubt there was another Gore leader at the time that would have supported this type of investigation and investment. Ritchie lived and breathed innovation and disruption. He had no fear of the unknown. Ritchie was not reckless, but he was willing to bet on a new business model. I now had two months to build a plan for a Gore-branded product. The clock was ticking.

The following is a short detour from my GLIDE Floss story.

I was called to jury duty a few years ago in Cleveland, Ohio. *Voir dire* is the process of questioning prospective jurors to see if there is cause for a juror not to serve. For this criminal matter, I was Juror #12, and I listened carefully to the questions directed to the first eleven prospective jurors as we sat in the jury box. The judge and the prosecution and defense attorneys' questions were friendly and designed to put a prospective juror at ease. I became confident I would not embarrass myself in *voir dire*. It is strange to sit in a jury box and be questioned by the prosecution and defense. My turn arrived, and the prosecutor's first question to me was a surprise. The prosecutor knew I was an attorney at Eaton, and I think he was putting me on the spot.

The prosecutor's question to me was, "What one word describes you?"

Think about it. What one word describes you? I got the correct answer, but there are no wrong answers. My response, after a few seconds, was "Lucky." I am lucky. Not lucky in winning lotteries or gambling, but I am persistent and always meet the right people at the right time to make good things happen.

Now back to the GLIDE Floss story.

In February 1991, I had two critical gaps in building a business plan to sell a branded dental floss to retail and dental professionals. The first gap was dental floss manufacturing. Gore is an expert in the manufacturing of high-technology fibers. But Gore had no experience applying a wax coating, spooling, injection molding of floss dispensers, cutting blades, and blister card packaging. My second gap is I did not know how to sell a product in drugstores and broader retail.

I immediately researched options for contract floss manufacturing and, by chance, found a reference to Gudebrod, Inc., located in Pottstown, Pennsylvania, only seventy miles away. This search was before the Internet made it easy to locate specialty companies. I introduced myself in a telephone call to Ed Johns, the president of Gudebrod. Gudebrod had manufactured dental floss for years earlier, but it was not a focus for the company. Gudebrod was a specialty fibers company. They had a single dental floss winder, and manufacturing still knew about spooling fiber and packaging. Gudebrod even had a two-piece dental floss dispenser and cutters for me to use in prototype dental floss. Within a month of meeting Ed Johns, I had a highly competent resource to manufacture GLIDE Floss product. Rapid prototyping was a gift, and I am lucky my path crossed with Ed Johns.

My second challenge was to gain a fundamental understanding of retail distribution and sales. I learned that merchandisers are responsible for retail product selection, placement, and store displays. I placed a cold call to the Vice President of Merchandising for Happy Harry's drugstores. Happy Harry's is a Delaware drugstore chain with about twenty-five stores at the time. Walgreens acquired Happy Harry's in 2006. I was surprised the Vice President gave me the time of day. Never underestimate a person's willingness to meet with you when you make a sincere request for help. I remember telling him that I was an engineer at Gore, responsible for developing a consumer dental floss product. I needed help in understanding retail sales for my business plan.

Meetings with Happy Harry's gave me valuable insight into sales to retailers. I had hundreds of questions. How are product decisions made? What is a high-impact product presentation? What are the best practices for blister-card packaging? What is the minimum unit sales by selling unit? Electronic ordering capability? Pricing and margin expectations? The best product promotions?

I was making good progress, and my first business plan was starting to take shape. Ritchie wanted results in ninety days, and I was not going to disappoint him. I could have easily spent six months or more learning the basics. Even with prototype manufacturing and a foundation in retail distribution, there were still many more questions than answers. A shortlist included fiber selection, product specification, and issues with blocking patents using wax in expanded PTFE fibers. I also needed to learn Class I medical device requirements, including Tripartite Biocompatibility Testing and drafting a Good Manufacturing Practice (GMP) for the manufacturing plant.

I also listed clinical testing, American Dental Association (ADA) Acceptable Seal, dispenser design, grassroots marketing plan, pricing, and retail testing, but these were future tasks.

I had lots of questions and was learning every day. How do you eat an elephant? One bite at a time. It took one year and nine months to develop and launch GLIDE Floss. I had first projected it would take nine months, and this seemed like a long time. I was a one-person team for the first fifteen months, but I was not alone. Hundreds of knowledgeable Gore Associates and suppliers helped me learn.

I conducted market research, learned about dental floss patents, literature searches, and attended the Chicago Dental Show to check out dental professional sales and see dental floss competition firsthand. Product specifications took longer than I expected, especially finalizing fiber denier and width specifications. Class 1 medical device requirements were a priority. I was drinking from the proverbial fire hose and having the time of my life.

The Business Plan and Review

There was no standard format for a business plan or a business review at Gore at the time. My approach was to keep it simple, and I created a three-year GLIDE Floss road map with six-month horizons. The business plan for the first year was mostly a series of tactics.

My GLIDE Floss business plan included:

- Product Description / Benefit

- Sales Opportunity

- Key Issues

- Technical and Regulatory Challenges

- Manufacturing Flow

- Grassroots Marketing

- Value Pricing

- 5-Year Sales and Margin Projections (No Cash Flow Modeling Yet)

As it turned out, most of the critical business assumptions in the plan were wrong. I projected a launch to drugstores in Q4 of 1991. We launched one year later. I guessed a suggested retail price of $2.25 for a 50-yard package of floss with blister-card packaging. I launched with a value price of $3.50 for a 50-meter package of floss. The year-five sales forecast was under $4M, with two full-time people managing the business. I was wrong, and GLIDE Floss was the #1 and #3 selling SKUs in just sixteen months. The plan assumed outsourcing dental floss manufacturing and packaging, customer service, sampling, and distribution to avoid hiring investments. The project promised an acceptable financial return, and I more than delivered on this forecast. It was just big enough to get a green light to proceed with building a product. I mentioned this could be a $50M-plus per year sales opportunity, but nobody believes this number in the first few months of product development.

Business plans can be beneficial or a waste of time. A boring plan is a summary of everything you know. This kind of business plan contains a lot of information, and at face value, it is impressive. It is all sizzle but no steak. The second type of business plan is the document that inspires. GLIDE Floss taught me the value of creating a business plan to drive the creative process. Decide what is valuable and when to be different. The strategy drives focus and choices.

The first business review of GLIDE Floss by Gore leaders was on April 16, 1991. I had never experienced such a challenging business review. Of course, this was my first business review, so the bar is not that high.

I worked with Ritchie to assemble the best leaders in Gore for the meeting, including Bob Gore. Bob was the Chairman and Chief Executive Officer of the company. Other attendees had built new businesses following Bob Gore's invention of expanded PTFE. Shanti Mehta was Gore's Chief Financial Officer (CFO), and he joined the meeting. Shanti had developed a summary of forms for five-year financial planning. I put these templates in a spreadsheet, and I was off to the races with financial modeling and sensitivity analysis. I will present more on this topic in Lesson 5.

The purpose of a business review is to get insight from experienced people who are open to new ideas. They will see gaps and help you ask better questions. I was not seeking approval to launch GLIDE Floss in the first review. Instead, I sought permission to develop the product and build a marketing plan for a Gore-branded dental floss product. I established a rhythm for GLIDE Floss reviews. The typical meeting time was two hours. I presented the business model, key activities, risks, and a five-year financial forecast focusing on variable cost analysis in the first fifteen to thirty minutes. The remaining time was an active discussion of six-month tactics, milestones, and threats (what, when, how, and the cost).

The first business review and subsequent reviews scheduled every six months were challenging and contentious. I participated in moot court competitions in law school, and the business review was like an appellate court hearing. My moot court experiences helped me. Attendees had many questions with minimal time to provide clear and crisp answers. Preparation is critical, and you must think on your feet.

My U.S. Naval Academy experience also helped me navigate an aggressive business review. The four acceptable responses for a first-year Naval Academy plebe are (1) "Yes, sir," (2) "No, sir," (3) "No excuse, sir," and (4) "I will find out, sir." At Gore, the three acceptable responses in a review were (1) "Yes," (2) "No," and (3) "I do not know, but I will find out." Never guess. The reviewers were experienced and practical. The first review was mainly concerned with the value of a Gore dental floss product and our lack of experience in consumer-packaged goods. We had data that indicated GLIDE Floss was not worth more than a 15% premium price. Reviewers were kind and did not make a big deal that I had no experience managing a product or running a business.

The first GLIDE Floss review ended similarly to my U.S. Navy interview for the Naval Nuclear Propulsion program with Admiral Hyman Rickover. Following interviews in Washington, D.C., focused on math, physics, and thermodynamics by the Admiral's staff, an aide to the Admiral directed me to Admiral Rickover's office. I had failed one of my three interviews during the day and was given a fourth staff interview before speaking with Admiral Rickover. Within seconds of meeting, Admiral Rickover concluded that I was not intelligent. I agreed with the Admiral that I was not smart, and I recall responding, "Yes, sir," a lot. He required me to study a minimum of twenty-five hours per week during my last semester at the Naval Academy. I agreed to a condition to write Admiral Rickover a weekly letter detailing my study time. The next thing I knew, Admiral Rickover looked to his aide and told him to get me out of his office in a dismissive tone. Immediately after leaving Admiral Rickover's office, the aide said, "That went well."

Like the Rickover interview, the first GLIDE Floss business review "went well." Gore leaders accepted my proposal to make investments in developing a Gore-branded consumer product for sale in leading drugstores. Mission accomplished.

The business review forced me to go faster in the first ninety days and focus. The discussion focused on weak links in my business plan, and I was better for it. One of the business review conditions was to gain buy-in from Gore's Medical Products Division, headquartered in Flagstaff, Arizona, to sell GLIDE Floss to dental professionals and retailers. I was in Gore's Industrial Sector that manufactured the fiber used in GLIDE Floss.

Consulting with the Medical Products Division would be a new adventure and a challenge. How do you launch a product when an existing Medical Division business considers your product low technology, negatively impacting their reputation and possibly decreasing sales?

The Clinical Trial

GLIDE Floss was disruptive at Gore. Most business leaders claim they like disruption, but they don't. Most managers prefer steady as she goes, with no surprises or uncertainty.

I immediately booked a flight to Flagstaff, Arizona, to spend a week with the Medical Products Division. After a few introductions, I met with the team most threatened by a Gore-branded dental floss. I have never met a more entrepreneurial and pleasant group of people. The leader of the team was Jeanne Ambruster. Jeanne is a natural leader who inspires people. Her business was at a critical stage in its launch of implantable products to periodontists. Her team invented using expanded PTFE to repair periodontal defects so that a tooth has more support and stability. The alternative to the procedure was to lose the tooth. Guided tissue regeneration is not lifesaving, but it is high technology.

Jeanne's schedule was crazy, but she still made time to meet with me. Her team confirmed my worst fears. GLIDE Floss was low technology in their world and not consistent with the GORE-TEX® brand they had built with periodontists. I argued that dental hygienists would recommend GLIDE Floss, and dentists would purchase samples for their patients and floss for their office use. Periodontists would not be a focus.

Regardless, her team was not supportive of my project, and they believed GLIDE Floss was a credible threat to their business reputation.

Jeanne's team was skilled in clinical trials, and they asked the obvious question: Does GLIDE Floss work as a dental floss? I did not know for sure. To date, everyone assumed GLIDE Floss worked. I had planned for GLIDE Floss to earn the American Dental Association (ADA) Acceptance seal, which requires a successful clinical trial by an independent organization. The clinical trial is straightforward and involves comparing a new floss to the leading dental floss that has already earned the ADA Acceptable Seal.

The Flagstaff team agreed that an independent clinical trial of GLIDE Floss would be the immediate focus, and results would influence their opinion. The good news was that this team had significant experience performing clinical trials with leading dental professionals and would help me get started. They suggested we approach Dr. Sebastian G. Ciancio, who led the Department of Periodontology at the State University of New York at Buffalo, New York. Dr. Ciancio is a recognized leader in the dental community.

A GLIDE Floss clinical evaluation was now my top priority. I needed support from the Flagstaff team, which was my path for product credibility. Jeanne's team scheduled a meeting with Dr. Ciancio for the following week. I liked the sense of urgency I shared with the Flagstaff team.

Dr. Ciancio is a gifted dentist and periodontist, and he is an amicable person. Our meeting began with a short introduction to my project and samples of prototype GLIDE Floss that met a new specification. Dr. Ciancio is also a curious individual and had many questions about my business plan, including grassroots marketing, pricing, and distribution.

After an hour or so of discussion, Dr. Ciancio became serious and offered his opinion that Gore launching a dental floss product would harm our Flagstaff team's reputation selling high technology membranes to treat periodontal disease. His concerns mirrored feedback I had heard from the

Flagstaff team the week before. I was surprised. I had made my best sales pitch, but he did not budge in his negative opinion. I left the meeting disappointed and returned to Maryland, wondering how to convince Dr. Ciancio that GLIDE Floss was a game-changer.

Then fate or luck took control. Dr. Ciancio called me the next day with an incredible story. He had taken GLIDE Floss samples home that evening and given them to his wife. She had tight contacts and did not like to floss. His wife immediately raved about GLIDE Floss, and Dr. Ciancio would be pleased to conduct a clinical evaluation. Thank you, Mrs. Ciancio.

The Flagstaff team accepted Dr. Ciancio's revised opinion and was anxious to understand whether the product worked. The clinical trial was a double-blind study that would include sixty people who did not floss. A control group of thirty people would use conventional dental floss daily that had earned the ADA Acceptance Seal. The test group would use GLIDE Floss. The patients were evaluated at weeks 0, 2, and 5 and scored for plaque index (P.I.), gingivitis (MGI), and interproximal bleeding sites (B.I.). At week 0, participants learned how to floss correctly.

The study was successful and determined no statistical difference existed between GLIDE Floss and conventional dental floss for P.I., MGI, and B.I. Perfect.

But it gets even better. During the clinical planning, I came up with an idea to extend the clinical trial to week 6. Following the final patient evaluation in week 5, the control group would use GLIDE Floss, and the GLIDE Floss test group would use conventional dental floss. At week 6, dentists again measured patients' P.I., MGI, and B.I., but the real purpose was a simple question: Which floss do you prefer? GLIDE Floss won over 74.5% of the participants, and only 25.5% chose conventional dental floss. Clinical results and the subjective preference data were persuasive to Gore leadership and dental professionals that GLIDE Floss was special.

The American Dental Association awarded GLIDE Floss the ADA Seal of Acceptance. The ADA Seal is a big deal for a new and disruptive product. Dr. Ciancio and his team published the clinical results in the International Journal of Clinical Preventive Dentistry, May-June 1992, Volume 14, Issue 3. This journal article's reprints were highly persuasive to dentists and hygienists suspicious of GLIDE Floss performance. I wish I had a dime for every dentist or hygienist who claimed the product did not work but changed their mind after being given a reprint of the study.

A few years later, I worked with Dr. Ciancio on a new clinical trial for GLIDE Floss. I was interested in promoting GLIDE Floss to teens. Do not be shocked. Teens do not floss. We conducted a similar blind study as the first clinical trial with sixty adolescents aged 13 to 18. None of the kids flossed. In this study, they were evaluated at weeks 0, 3, 6, and 9 and again scored for plaque index (P.I.), gingivitis (MGI), and interproximal bleeding sites (B.I.). We asked the teens to keep a daily diary of brushing and flossing. At week 6, the teens in the control group used GLIDE Floss, and the test group switched to conventional dental floss. At week 9, the preference results showed adolescents could be motivated to use dental floss and preferred GLIDE Floss. The adolescent study was a second successful clinical trial.

I cannot remember why, but we included a second control group in this study of thirty kids who did not floss, and participants recorded their daily oral hygiene practices with no changes. There was a surprise with the second control group. They experienced the same improvement in P.I., MGI, and B.I. as the control group and test group "with no change in their oral hygiene practices." We decided to conduct an additional interview with the third control group patients. The kids cheated. The students discussed the study with their peers in the control and test groups and decided they would floss daily, so their oral hygiene results would be good. Can you imagine kids suddenly concerned with oral health, and they flossed?

I had read of the "Hawthorne Effect" on productivity assessments in my manufacturing leadership days. The name comes from a research test conducted at the Hawthorne Works manufacturing plant. That test concluded that better lighting resulted in improved worker productivity. The reality is that the workers knew their activities were under scrutiny, and they worked more diligently while being closely monitored. Improved lighting had nothing to do with their productivity increases. The Hawthorne Effect is real. People would change their behavior if they knew they were being watched.

The second clinical study was still a success since we had a control and test group of teens. Leadership fired me from the

GLIDE Floss business before I had the opportunity to use the second clinical study in a grassroots marketing program.

Grassroots Marketing & Happy Harry's

I met with dental hygienists at local dental professional meetings in Delaware, Maryland, and Pennsylvania for months. I positioned GLIDE Floss samples as an experimental product and welcomed their feedback. Hygienists are not shy, and I learned how to tune the GLIDE Floss value proposition from their perspective. I was using the Gudebrod two-piece round dispenser for the prototype product. Dental hygienists loved the floss, but most did not care for the two-piece round dispenser. It was awkward to open and close compared to a one-piece dispenser. An improved floss dispenser was a must.

I was anxious to conduct a retail sales test in drugstores to challenge pricing assumptions and confirm my grassroots marketing strategy. Specifically, would dental hygienists refer their patients to stores to buy the product? The retail trial could not wait for the availability of a new dispenser.

My relationship with Happy Harry's drugstores in Delaware was excellent, and I asked the V.P. of Merchandising to sponsor a three-month retail beta test. A product trial is a big deal for a retailer. Adding products for sale means other products go away. It takes planning. Selling a prototype product poses a reputation risk, and I am grateful Happy Harry's supported the trial. Gore did not charge Happy Harry's for the beta product, and they did not charge Gore a placement fee. I suggested a retail price of $2.99 for a 50-yard dispenser packaged on a blister card. I assumed GLIDE Floss was worth $2.25 for a 50-yard dispenser, so I went high on price. The leading brand of conventional floss sold for $1.40 for a 50-yard dispenser in Happy Harry's twenty-five stores.

I worked with a local marketing agency on a GLIDE Floss logo and a blister card package.

Developing the beta test blister card is a good memory and my first retail packaging experience. I had requested the marketing agency create a blister card that stood out from the crowd. In our first meeting, the agency presented a lineup of bright orange background blister cards. They did stand out, and I guess the orange blister cards were what I had requested. Rather than screaming technology and quality, they resembled a Halloween graphic or maybe a laundry detergent. I rejected the effort and suggested a dark blue primary color on a gray background would be a better look. The next round of blister card concepts was much better. The logo was a bit shaky, but the gray background appeared to be a tasteful bathroom tile. We featured the Gore company logo on the front and the back of the card.

I used the two-piece round dispenser from Gudebrod with a couple of improvements. I substituted polystyrene for the white polypropylene to give the dispenser a firm feel. The insert holding the blade was made of transparent light blue polystyrene to easily view the quantity of floss in the dispenser. I'm not too fond of the surprise of pulling the last four inches of floss from the dispenser, and I became somewhat obsessed with a viewing window in future dental floss dispenser designs.

We began the twelve-week retail sales test in January 1992. We offered two stock-keeping units (SKUs) for sale, regular and mint flavor, 50-yards. My goal was to match unit sales of the leading brand of conventional floss SKU, and I first guessed this would be thousands of units in twelve weeks. I was wrong. The sales objective was one unit per store per week per SKU, just 600 packages in twelve weeks.

At the beginning of the test, I mailed GLIDE Floss samples to all Delaware dental hygienists, sent additional samples to dental offices, and advised them that GLIDE Floss was available in Happy Harry's. In addition, I included a homemade handout for hygienists to give to patients that referred them to Happy Harry's drugstores to buy GLIDE Floss.

Remember, the goal was to sell 600 packages in twelve weeks.

At the end of the twelve weeks, we sold more than 12,000 units. Yes, 12,000 units. About 60% mint and 40% unflavored.

During this trial, I spent most of my time working with Gudebrod to manufacture the product and then deliver the product from Gudebrod several times a week to Happy Harry's distribution center to keep up with demand. In addition, Gudebrod was scaling up manufacturing with new winders and packaging equipment in preparation for a national launch later in the year.

I do not know how much GLIDE Floss would have been sold during the trial if stores could keep the product fully stocked. Thousands of more units, for sure.

I call this a successful test, and I confirmed the effectiveness of grassroots marketing with dental hygienists as my reference set.

I was pleased with test sales, but the results were confusing. Was our price too low? Maybe Delaware consumers were biased to support a local company? Were consumers hoarding and buying multiple units at a time? I had been meeting with Delaware dental hygienists for months. Maybe they just liked me or took pity on me? During the trial, I joked that it took me a lot of time and personal expense to drive to all the Happy Harry's stores in Delaware and personally buy 12,000 units of floss.

I ran a single advertisement in *Delaware Today magazine* in the trial's final month just for kicks and learning. It is tough to measure the impact of a print advertisement, but I do not believe it significantly affected sales. I was already planning on sampling dental hygienists as the primary marketing investment for GLIDE Floss. I had learned that most retailers expect print advertising for new products. I like being different, but you need to decide when to be different. For the national launch, I had a modest budget for print advertisements' limited placement. The print advertising's real value was providing reprints of the ads with sales materials to retailers. Including three or four ad reprints in a retailer mailing suggests a broad and expensive print advertising campaign.

My communication with Gore leadership was simple. We demonstrated that GLIDE Floss is a winner. It is worth at least $2.99 for 50-yards. Ritchie suggested we go metric for our launch, and he proposed a 50-meter (54.7-yards) package. I liked it, and I suggested a price of $3.50 per SKU. My guess was GLIDE Floss was worth $4 to $5 to the customer over conventional dental floss with a value of $1.40 per SKU.

I dismissed concerns that I could not explain 12,000-plus unit sales. If real sales potential was 50% lower than actual sales, we sold 6,000 units with a target of 600 units. How about 75% lower and we sold 3,000 units. Sales were off the chart and encouraging. I concluded that dental hygienists loved the product, and the grassroots marketing strategy worked.

Grassroots marketing included (1) ongoing sampling of GLIDE Floss to dental hygienists, (2) advising hygienists where patients could buy the product, (3) politely asking hygienists and their patients to request local retailers stock GLIDE Floss, (4) sales of GLIDE Floss designed for the dental practice for patient awareness, and (5) limited dental professional and consumer print advertising. More than 80% of marketing investments were sampling.

The Happy Harry's retail test identified two critical actions: (1) prioritize developing the improved dispenser and (2) work with the marketing agency on an improved GLIDE Floss logo.

I launched GLIDE Floss in October 1992, and Happy Harry's continued offering the test product until the launch. Unit sales of both SKUs continued to sell more than double the leading brand of conventional dental floss at more than twice the price. Thank you to the dental hygienists in Delaware who recommended the product to their patients.

I had worked on GLIDE Floss for fifteen months at the end of the retail trial. The success of the clinical evaluation and the retail test was compelling. Business reviews by business leaders continued to be challenging, and some were still skeptical. Do not worry about skeptics. It is less risky to be a skeptic than be an active supporter of a highly disruptive product. GLIDE Floss had many skeptics, but they did not suggest stopping the project. I also had ongoing enthusiastic support and coaching from Ritchie Snyder. Reasonable investments continued.

A New Floss Dispenser

I have only met a couple of people in my life who overwhelm me with their inspiration and vision. In my ELIXIR Strings story, I will introduce you to Dave Myers. Dave is an innovator and a one-of-a-kind visionary. Maybe I am just a bit jealous of Dave?

My success in product launches comes from working hard and not dropping too many balls. Still, I will take credit for being inspired by two decisions in developing GLIDE Floss. The first was to propose Gore sell a branded consumer product direct to retail. Gore selling a branded product was a radical idea and, in twenty years, had not been a viable alternative. My second example of inspiration is the design of the GLIDE Floss dispenser. It is a great design, and I am proud of the dispenser.

I began designing a new floss dispenser in October 1991 by collecting every dental floss dispenser I could find. I gathered more than twenty commercial floss dispensers and then made a list of what I liked and did not want for each dispenser. For example, all the dispensers had sharp edges. I preferred a rounded edge and knew it would stand out compared to the competition. Most of the dispensers were designed to hold more than 100 yards and were a bit clunky. A slighter profile offered a premium look. Several dispensers had a cut-out in the plastic to view the floss quantity. Nice, but not very functional. I was obsessed with quickly seeing the amount of floss. The better dispensers had a one-piece, two-hinge design, and I copied this feature. Why reinvent the wheel? It was a standard feature. I wanted the dispenser to seal and protect the floss. Finally, I worked closely with a Gore patent attorney to understand intellectual property opportunities.

My next step was to make sketches of dispenser concepts. My colleagues know that I carry a straight edge wherever I go, and it is a habit from law school. I am old and went to law school before notebook computers existed. I was an excellent note-taker in classes, but I found I could not read some of my notes with my small script handwriting at the lectures' paces. I discovered I could use a straight edge and print my notes in block letters faster than cursive writing, and they were always legible. It is not likely that a person who carries a straight edge for block lettering is a creative designer, but this did not stop me.

By November, I had a decent personal sketch of the new dispenser, and I hired a local marketing company graphic artist to create a professional drawing of my concept. Since January, Ed Johns, the president of Gudebrod, had become a mentor to me. I took the dispenser sketches to one of our meetings, and we brainstormed how to view the quantity of floss. Together we came up with the idea of a polystyrene window that would also serve as the post for the floss bobbin. There are three issued GLIDE Floss dispenser patents. One design patent with the floss container closed and another design patent with the floss dispenser open. Ed Johns is a co-inventor of the combined post and lens in the GLIDE Floss dispenser.

Ed Johns then referred me to a company that designed baby strollers for the next step in building a dispenser. Go figure, a baby stroller company. The company had significant expertise in building single-cavity prototype molds to make plastic stroller components. Their design engineer was excited to work on a new floss dispenser mold with me. I learned that my preferred rounded edge was too round to be practical. But my sketches were adequate for mold design drawings. Within a few weeks, the company had made a single-cavity prototype dispenser mold. I generally prefer working with smaller companies than larger companies when I need help and have tight schedules. If competent, they are fast and responsive. My bet is a traditional molder would have required a few months, not weeks, to build a prototype tool.

The biggest challenges with the single-cavity prototype mold were the snap and hinge improvements for secure closure during manufacturing. By March 1992, the company had improved the single-cavity mold and manufactured prototype dispensers that worked. I immediately placed a purchase order with a larger injection molding company to build an eight-cavity production tool for August delivery. The clinical evaluation and the production tool were the two significant investments I had made during product development.

It has been almost thirty years, and the GLIDE Floss dispenser is unchanged and a big part of the brand. The dispenser is a fantastic design for a guy who writes block text with a straight edge.

The First Hire

It is April 1992, and I desperately need help. I was a one-person show for fifteen months, getting help here and there from many people. I am planning a national launch for dental professionals and drugstores. I received approval to hire a full-time salesperson to join the team, and I suggested that the perfect person would be a dental hygienist. I was impressed by so many of the dental hygienists I had met during the past year.

The job posting was unusual. It included dental professional marketing and retail sales responsibilities, plus the requirement of "doing whatever is necessary for the business's success." The interview team settled on two candidates. One was an experienced hygienist and the other a hygienist who had just graduated the previous year with a B.S. from the University of Maryland's dental school.

The safe bet was to hire an experienced hygienist. But I thought the new hygienist would be more flexible in work responsibilities, and we made an offer. It was a lucky day for me when Jane Gardner, née Delp, joined the GLIDE Floss team. I was not alone anymore, and we are a great team.

Jane and I had six months to make final plans for a national launch. Jane focused more on the dental professional program, and I focused more on retail. I still remember Jane in the plant packing samples for hygienists, taking inventories, and making calls to dental associations regarding upcoming meetings.

I am so thankful Jane joined GLIDE Floss, and I had the privilege to work with Jane on ELIXIR Strings, and in a future Fabrics Division project I refer to as the "Barn Coat." I talked with Jane a few months ago on the telephone, and she commented that we always knew we would succeed. Failure was not an option. Today, Jane works in Human Resources and recruits the next generation of leaders for Gore.

Product Launch — Grassroots Success

You would think a product launch would be a massive deal with bells, whistles, fireworks, speeches, and hoopla. The GLIDE Floss launch was relatively quiet.

My experience is that a good product launch is like painting a room, 90% preparation. It is October 1992, and we traveled to Orlando, Florida, for the American Dental Association's annual meeting to launch GLIDE Floss. Before the trade show, we had sampled dental hygienists and invited them to our booth. We also sent samples to dental offices and, again, let them know our booth number. I placed an advertisement in the ADA's dental professional journal that month. It was a retro-looking advertisement with the title "Great Advances in Dental Care" and featured six dental artifacts in filtered black and white pictures from 1844 to 1942. A photo of GLIDE Floss is in color with the date 1992. Not my best effort, but it was okay.

My sister Priscilla and her husband Gary joined Jane and me in the booth, and it was an exhausting event. We had steady to crazy crowds in front of our ten-foot booth for three days. I believe in tight budgets, and we borrowed a trade show booth from another business. I recall we recovered from the first day in the hotel jacuzzi and then repeated non-stop engagements with hygienists for two more days. We created a buzz.

During the previous six months, Jane and I developed a GLIDE Floss products portfolio for sale to dental professionals that included 200-meter office font refills, a 200-meter vial dispenser for office use, and five or ten-meter trial packages to give to patients. Our professional products featured a subtle Times Roman font logo. I used a tin dispenser from the 1920s for the five-meter patient samples. It was about the size of a quarter and fit nicely in your pocket. We also featured our new fifty-meter consumer products in regular and mint flavor with a fresh new consumer logo. I proudly displayed the Gore logo.

The GLIDE Floss retail launch was simple. Jane and I prioritized the leading drugstores and mass merchants. Grocery stores would not have priority in Year 1. Our calls to chain retailers for appointments mainly went unanswered. Welcome to sales. But most of the retailers had an "open call" one day of the month. These are perfect sales call opportunities for a new product. You show up at 7:00 a.m. or earlier and sign in on a first-come basis to see a buyer. You sit most of the day in a waiting room and then get five to ten minutes to make a sales pitch. Jane and I learned to be crisp communicators.

We led with our sales performance with Happy Harry's and made offers to mail samples to every dental hygienist located within a particular zip code of their stores to let them know of availability. Similarly, every dental hygienist mailing requested they refer their patients to the retailer to purchase GLIDE Floss.

It worked!

Ongoing focus on sampling dental hygienists and asking them to request retailers to offer the product was an overwhelming success. Beware. You cannot sample one time and expect results. Our program worked because the core sampling program and communication to dental hygienists were ongoing. Our sampling program and attendance at professional events allowed us to develop relationships with thousands of dental hygienists. Plus, we had a great product.

By the end of 1993, GLIDE Floss was available in over sixty retail chains across the country, including the leading drugstore chains and mass merchants. In February 1994, GLIDE Floss was the #1 (mint) and #3 (unflavored) bestselling SKUs in the United States. We expanded our team in 1993 and 1994 with exceptional sales, customer service, and engineering capability. The five sales associates I hired in the GLIDE Floss business were all dental hygienists. They focused on dental professional and retailer sales. GLIDE Floss was profitable within six months of product launch, and profits paid for the investment by February 1994.

In 1994, we finally hired our second sales associate. Jane Gardner and I were still calling on all the USA chain retailers. We were overdue to expand our sales team, and we needed to focus on grocery store chain distribution. We also desperately needed a person on the west coast to manage drugstore chain relationships and lead west coast dental professional meetings. We got lucky and hired Janifer Brown, née White, a practicing dental hygienist in Seattle. Janifer is one of the most incredible people I have ever met. Hardworking, passionate, detailed, and a self-starter. I could never keep up with Janifer, and like Jane Gardner, she was crucial to the success of the GLIDE Floss launch and its longer-term sustainability. Janifer has an exquisite sense of humor, a positive attitude, and high standards. Again, we were lucky to find Janifer in our candidate search limited to dental hygienists.

The Downside

Jane and I pulled off a national product launch with just two full-time people. But all was not good. Jane traveled non-stop to dental meetings and supported retail sales calls for nearly two years. She had zero work-life balance. I was also flying non-stop with sales calls, managing production, marketing, and other duties. We were stretched too thin, and it does not have to be this way.

The hectic pace, project challenges, and stress of the past eighteen months began taking a toll on my health. I was mostly successful in hiding it from my co-workers. The truth is, I felt my health issues were a weakness. I first experienced gastroesophageal reflux, where you feel like you have food stuck in your throat and swallowing is impossible. I had trouble eating at restaurants on many occasions due to this condition. But wait, there is more. My next health issue was a range of severe and unexplained allergies. On several occasions, I went to the emergency room due to my throat swelling and an inability to breathe. It is impressive to watch emergency room staff react to a person who has difficulty breathing. They are quick to respond. Also, without warning, my lips would swell to the size of a golf ball. The swelling would subside in about twenty-four hours. I spent time with an allergist and confirmed allergies to various food items from tomatoes, barley, and shellfish. Sleep was becoming a problem.

In hindsight, I should have set a more modest pace for the product launch, or better yet, convinced my leadership to hire additional people and build a team to share the load. Building a team committed to success has been my strategy for all projects going forward. I learned the hard way to manage my stress better. We hired competent people for the GLIDE Floss team, and my health improved. Today, I have no allergies or swelling of my lips. I manage my gastroesophageal reflux. I still set challenging goals and sometimes err on the side of doing too much. It is just my nature.

The moral of this part of the story is never to work so hard that it impacts your mental or physical health. Take care of yourself.

Expanded Products and Geography

Enough about me, what do you think about me? Just kidding. Back to the GLIDE Floss story. Sales in the USA were exceptional, and the team began expanding our product portfolio. A successful hire to the team was John Dolan as our lead research and product engineer. John had worked on several GLIDE Floss projects, and I liked his desire to understand the market and his focus on creating new sales opportunities. After joining the team full-time, John worked closely with me on many product improvements and inventions. The truth is, John was the brains of our collaboration for most of our efforts. He is an intelligent guy. John was key to developing many product improvements, including but not limited to an improved dental floss fiber, a new dental floss dispenser, a dental floss holder, a single-unit flossing apparatus, a new vial dispenser, a combined flosser, dental tape, and a new floss dispensing device. John and I worked closely with David Johns, our patent and trademark attorney. The team's entrepreneurial spirit was alive and well as we achieved sales success.

In 1994, I began evaluating the sale of GLIDE Floss in new geographies. One of the first countries I researched was Brazil. I planned a two-week visit to a dental conference in Sao Paulo. During this trip, I learned that people in Brazil are friendly and that dental hygienists in Brazil influence preventive dental care like dental hygienists in the United States. I visited every retailer that offered dental floss for sale. Did you know Sao Paulo has the best grocery stores in the world? They do. The quantity and quality of produce and fresh fish were beyond belief.

I identified thirty retailers to visit on the trip and hired a driver to take me from store to store. You do not want to drive in Sao Paulo if you are a visitor to the country. There are dangerous neighborhoods that you must avoid. After the second day of visiting stores, the driver turned to me and said, "Please. Let me help you." He was sincere in his request, and I was confused. I asked what he meant, and he explained, "Please tell me what you are looking for, and I can take you to the right store to find it." He was a nice guy. When visiting stores, I asked permission to take pictures of the floss display, and most retailers approved. My takeaway from the Sao Paulo field trip was that the Brazil dental floss market was too crowded, just like the United States. Brazil is a perfect environment to introduce GLIDE Floss with a grassroots marketing plan like the United States.

People in the United States and Brazil know they should floss, but most do not make it a part of their daily routine. Some people just cannot be bothered, but many people have tight contacts that shred conventional nylon floss, and the floss snaps painfully into their gums. Remember my product value proposition: GLIDE Floss slides easily between tight contacts without shredding. My Brazil trip also established a best practice to get out of the office and learn from seeing products and meeting people. Use the Internet to search for the background, not the strategy and action plan.

I made a similar trip to Germany to assess sales opportunities. Flossing in Germany was quite a bit different than in the United States or Brazil. Do not get me wrong. Germany is a beautiful place to visit, especially Bavaria. I learned that dental hygienists were not widespread, and generally, there was little focus on preventive care. Most leading retailers typically offered a single nylon floss option, and dental picks were popular. Dental picks are made of wood and look like a toothpick. It was almost the opposite of the United States and Brazil. In Germany, flossing was not a priority. I worked with a local team, and we brainstormed a different approach to drive sales. We determined health-conscious women were more likely open to the need to floss daily. Our first marketing campaign would educate nurses in Bavaria about the benefits of flossing. I would expand the program if successful. The team began our program by mailing a sample to nurses with an educational brochure. The nurses could buy the product direct from Gore, and we asked them to request local pharmacies to purchase the product. Selling a new product that requires a behavior change is a red flag. Success, if achieved, will take a lot of time and investment. Still, the program would rely on grassroots communication with health-conscious women.

I was fired from the GLIDE Floss team before I understood whether we built a good strategy in Brazil or Germany. Still, I was pleased to take the necessary time to learn the market versus copying the United States business plan.

Intellectual Property

A broad portfolio of intellectual property is outstanding unless it is not. All the engineers are freaking out right now. I am proud of the patents, brand, and trade secrets created in

GLIDE Floss's launch. Just remember that patents are only good if they result in profitable sales.

I had a secret weapon for maximizing the GLIDE Floss intellectual property value. His name is David Johns, and he is an exceptional attorney. Someday, I need to write a complete profile of David Johns, and he will serve as an example for all corporate attorneys to emulate. I am not kidding or just trying to inflate David's abilities. The key to David's success is his passion for innovation. He loves it and enjoys teaching the broader team best practices to build a valuable intellectual property portfolio.

Intellectual property is not valuable if it does not contribute to profitable sales. It is not complicated. My name is on twelve dental floss-related patents. I do not think I am an inventor, more of a problem-solver. I have learned that the most valuable inventions solve a problem.

Two Misses

I must remind myself to focus. I admit that I can be distracted by a new, shiny object. Another weakness I manage is my belief that I can do more than time allows. Focus is critical in a product launch and running a business.

I pitched two dental floss products to leadership that did not receive approval to launch. I include this section just in case you have the impression that everything went my way for GLIDE Floss.

I refer to the first missed product as "duet floss." I do not like using GLIDE Floss, and I have used cheap nylon dental floss since I was eighteen. Remember, GLIDE Floss slides easily between tight teeth without shredding. My contacts are not tight. The best dental floss in the world combines conventional nylon dental floss with GLIDE Floss. This product is duet floss. It even looked cool. Imagine three-parts green nylon fiber entangled with one-part expanded PTFE fiber combined with a refreshing mint flavor. It had the scrubbing feel of nylon and slides more easily between contacts than conventional dental floss. It was not as good as GLIDE Floss for shredding or sliding between close contacts but seemed much better than traditional dental floss. The expanded PTFE fiber was a much lower denier than GLIDE Floss, and its sole purpose was to provide improved lubrication.

Leadership asked whether duet floss would cannibalize GLIDE Floss sales? Who knows? I was okay with cannibalized sales so long as Gore made the sale of duet floss, and the margins were equal to or maybe even better than GLIDE Floss. Gore's second concern is duet floss would give nylon credibility as a higher technology floss. Duet floss includes high technology expanded PTFE fiber for product differentiation. My idea of pursuing duet floss came just after the GLIDE Floss launch, and it was fair for leadership to remind me to focus on the GLIDE Floss launch. By mid-1994, I thought we had the bandwidth to pursue duet floss, but my proposed investments were dead on arrival. I regret that duet floss never made it to the market. I also regret not manufacturing a lifetime supply of this special dental floss for personal use.

I want it all.

I first deleted the previous sentence stating, "I want it all," since I knew the antitrust enthusiasts would immediately freak out. Then, I added it back for me to deliver an antitrust warning. Early in my career, I learned that you never confess or put in writing a desire to dominate the market, wanting it all, crushing the competition, driving companies out of business, or having similar objectives. Did I say never? If you achieve a dominant position in the market, then these statements will haunt you.

We missed the opportunity to pursue private label expanded PTFE high technology dental floss. Private label product is a retail store-branded version of GLIDE Floss featuring Gore fiber. I knew GLIDE Floss's success would result in knockoffs with store brands. Why not be the guy knocking off GLIDE Floss? Another benefit is private label product further builds a relationship with the retailer. In 1994, I mistakenly thought I had buy-in to develop a store-branded floss launch plan. I created a single-cavity prototype tool for a new floss dispenser that kind of looked like the GLIDE Floss dispenser. It was an excellent dispenser but did not have a window to see floss quantity. A leadership team reviewed the product, and I had no support for this idea. The team would continue to focus on GLIDE Floss and new GLIDE Floss product introductions. As expected, store-branded knockoffs of GLIDE Floss were on the shelves by 1995.

I want it all.

In mid-1995, I worked on making an improved toothbrush using Gore technology. I was beginning to feel comfortable with toothbrush design, performance, and manufacturing when the end arrived.

The End – You Are Fired

It was morning in October 1995, and Ritchie asked me to come to his office. On arrival, I was given a memorandum and told that I was fired from the GLIDE Floss team effective immediately. I would meet with Ritchie the next day to discuss my Gore future. I went home. It was a beautiful day in October, and I recall enjoying a nice bike ride that afternoon with my wife.

So, what happened?

I know that I have earned a mixed reputation as a leader. My passion, urgency, and drive for excellence can be challenging for people who prefer a less dynamic work environment. I have high expectations for myself and my colleagues. Mistakes are okay if we learn from them. Transparency and ethical behavior are a must. No secrets. I have no time for idiots or foolish behavior. I know that I am far from perfect, but my intentions are good. Seriously. I have learned that my leadership style and passion can be intimidating to some people.

I previously mentioned that my sister, Priscilla, is a dental hygienist. Priscilla was an immediate fan of GLIDE Floss and encouraged me to make dental hygienists the focus of our marketing and communication plan. Dental hygienists continued to be the focus of our grassroots marketing plan in

1995. We divided the USA into eleven regions, and we identified annual dental shows and hygienist meetings by date and region. The team mailed samples to dental hygienists before the event, and we invited them to stop by our booth to show them our latest product innovation.

I always included my name and home address in dental professional mailings to assess the timing and the quality of the communication. You can learn a lot by evaluating an actual sample delivered to your mailbox.

I had received a GLIDE Floss sample two days before being fired. This mailing to dental hygienists was to include a broad array of floss products. Instead, I receive an extra-large bubble envelope with a single dispenser of floss and a letter inviting me to visit the GLIDE Floss booth at an upcoming dental meeting. I was confused and upset by such a cheap and wasteful mailing. The next day, I learned that a team member had modified our sampling program due to challenges with fiber supply. No one told me. I read the team member the riot act for making this decision without me.

I was fired the following day from the GLIDE Floss team.

I did not learn a thing from being fired from the GLIDE Floss team. Nothing. I would not behave any differently given the same situation. My passion for engaging dental hygienists in a grassroots strategy had made GLIDE Floss a success. Sending out second-rate mailings to thousands of hygienists without discussion would never be acceptable. A better solution with fiber supply limitations was to delay mailings.

I have learned that sometimes life is not fair. You then have a choice of being angry and resentful, or you can move forward to seek new challenges. I chose to move on, but I am still angry and bitter about losing my job.

Ritchie provided me assurances that all would be well for me at Gore. My wife and I went to Jane Gardner's wedding the weekend after being fired, and Ritchie was in attendance. Ritchie made a point of engaging privately with my wife, Pamela. He and Pam took a quiet walk on the grounds of the country club setting for about twenty minutes. His message to Pamela was not to worry. Ritchie told Pam there would be other opportunities for me in the company.

I will always be sad about being fired from the GLIDE Floss business. Did I mention it was not fair? There were so many opportunities to expand distribution globally and launch complementary products. It was a great job, and we had hired an incredible team of people.

But, being fired from the GLIDE Floss team was one of the luckiest days of my life.

Epilogue – It Seems Weird

I kept in touch with many of my GLIDE Floss teammates over the years and recruited several to help me with difficult startups. Otherwise, I had no contact with the GLIDE Floss business, and this seems weird. I had an office in the same building, but I might as well have left the company.

In April 1997, I accepted a Gore "Produck Award" for GLIDE Floss from Bob Gore at a company leadership meeting.

The "Produck Award" initiative was started in 1987 by Gore leadership to recognize innovation and disruption in new products featuring Gore technology. The award was a hand-carved wooden duck decoy relegated to a display cabinet in the plant cafeteria. I am sure you caught the play on words between a duck decoy and a product = produck. Bob referred to me as "Mr. Product Introduction" in his comments, which is a great compliment. I was surprised that the leadership requested me to accept the award since GLIDE Floss leadership was in attendance. The award presentation and the follow-up front-page article in a Gore newspaper felt weird. For two years, the GLIDE Floss team excluded me from any association with the product.

In September 2003, the Procter & Gamble Company announced the agreement to acquire Gore's GLIDE Floss brand. Like most acquisitions, the terms of the sale by P&G were not disclosed. I was not aware Gore was engaged with P&G to sell the GLIDE Floss business, and I have no insider information. I do have confidence in Gore's leadership and that the divestiture was an excellent business decision.

An excellent business decision is sad from my perspective. I worked in corporate development and targeted companies for acquisitions for ten years. I never knew a company to sell a growing business with high margins and a pipeline of innovative products. Companies typically sell businesses that are declining or do not perceive they have a path for continued success. I was given a small financial award following the sale of GLIDE Floss, and the Gore leader thanked me for being an early member of the team. No mention of leading the launch for five years of my life. And here I thought I was the only member of the team for the first fifteen months and was the inventor on the patents delivering high sales? This seemed weird.

My bet is the GLIDE Floss leadership team failed to innovate, failed to sell a vision, and the result in 2003 was Gore leadership selling the business. I could be wrong, just my guess. Selling the GLIDE Floss business seems weird because of the hundreds of new dental floss ideas we had and our passion for expanding sales globally. Innovation was the foundation of the GLIDE Floss business. To me, the sale of the business is sad and likely an excellent business decision.

Story 2. ELIXIR Strings

The Idea

Dave Myers is the most innovative person I have ever met. He has an exceptional ability to see opportunities and solve problems. One of my future schemes is to develop a television show based on Dave. He had over fifty patents while working at Gore, and Dave's patents make for exciting stories with diverse characters and even some villains. I am confident this television show would be a huge hit.

Dave is intriguing because he does not fit an engineer or scientist's stereotype. He is soft-spoken, straightforward, ridiculously modest, and relentlessly focused on making life better through technology. Dave graduated from the University of Northern Arizona with a teaching degree. Dave looks like an elementary school teacher rather than some mad scientist in the laboratory. Dave is also unique because his natural mechanical skills enable him to build any product he envisions. Dave can make a bike cable, a catheter, a guitar string, a vascular graft, or rebuild a railroad speeder. Experienced mechanics would be envious of his home shop.

Dave is also practical, which is rare with gifted people. Dave does not count patents. When I first met Dave in October 1995, he explained he had one priority for his inventions: Products must be successfully launched and offer a better experience for the user. Dave's success metrics were product sales, margins, and profit. Most inventors I know brag about filing a patent as compared to sales. Not Dave.

The path to the idea of a better guitar string had a curious journey. In 1990, Dave worked on a project to develop an improved catheter guidewire. In this invention, Dave created a guidewire with a fluoropolymer tape covering. The covering allowed the guidewire to tolerate the application of greater force before uncoiling and wire breakage. The catheter work led Dave to invent an improved control cable in 1991 used for bicycle shift and brake cables. In the 1990s, Gore launched RIDE-ON® cable systems. What a great brand name. It is the summer of 1995, and Dave is developing improved actuation cables for puppets. The team used a wound guitar string for a push-pull cable with a fluoropolymer covering.

Dave asked the question, "Could this push-pull cable be a better guitar string?"

Dave and his team made prototypes of acoustic guitar strings after his query. The prototypes were given to a local high school guitar club for evaluation and became affectionately known as the "High School String." The strings were popular with the high school club, and amateur musician feedback was encouraging. Dave is an intelligent guy. He quickly makes prototypes of any new idea to test the concept. He is not looking for a commercial product but assessing whether the concept is worthy of more time. Today, this is a "minimum viable product" or "MVP," but Dave successfully practiced this concept long before it had a title.

Our patent and trademark attorney, David Johns, had a sample of the "High School String" and showed them to Bob Gore, Chairman and Chief Executive Officer, and Ritchie Snyder, Industrial Division Leader, while on business travel.

By coincidence, I had recently been fired from the GLIDE Floss team. Ritchie suggested I introduce myself to Dave Myers during a scheduled trip to Flagstaff and discuss his idea for an improved guitar string. Just as one door was closing, another door opened for me. I met with Dave in October 1995, and I knew within five minutes that I wanted to work with him. He is passionate, enthusiastic, and realistic at the same time.

As a transition from GLIDE Floss, I had the opportunity to work on a logistics project in the Medical Products Division for six months. I would investigate guitar strings with Dave on the side. Most people know being a "project person" in a corporation is an invitation to refresh your resume and look for new employment. Now I am a project person, which seems better than being unemployed. At least it was an exciting project. I worked closely with key members of the Medical Products sales team to reinvent a consignment system for GORE-TEX vascular grafts in hospitals. It is a real problem and customer-focused. The negative financial impact on Gore was growing.

Vascular grafts and other Gore devices had to be immediately available at the hospital for surgeries. Grafts expire, and it is crucial to use grafts before expiration. Purchasing at hospitals was not organized to make this happen consistently, and it was not unusual for Gore consignment products to expire before use. Then, Gore is on the hook for the cost of the expired product.

I was lucky to be assigned a cubicle next to Jeannie Guthrie, née Mayer, at the Medical West plant. Jeannie was a financial leader in Medical Products, and I needed her help to quantify the expired vascular graft cost impact to Gore and calculate the return on possible solutions. Jeannie was an expert in our Medical Products; she knew the sales team, and within a month, she became my partner in the project. Jeannie is hands-on, and we traveled to hospitals to learn firsthand the problem and develop solutions. We came up with an innovative vending option to manage consignment inventory that used the latest computer laptops, product barcodes, and wireless capability to track inventory and product expiration dates. It was an excellent system that worked.

My day job was in Medical Products consignment inventory, and I worked nights and weekends to learn the guitar string market. At first, I was suspicious of Gore selling a coated guitar string. I became excited as I learned more about the opportunity, musician frustration with the limited life of a conventional guitar string, and the opportunity for disruption in a new market for Gore. Leading GLIDE Floss's startup made me more thoughtful, and I immediately began assembling a guitar string business plan. Within a few months, I scheduled time with Dave to review a first draft business plan. I needed Dave's support to transition from my logistics project to work on guitar strings full-time.

I was ready to commit to making guitar strings a successful business at Gore. Dave appreciated the work I did to outline the market opportunity, value proposition, communication with musicians and retailers, a grassroots product marketing strategy, value pricing concepts, and distribution options. We agreed I would engage with Ritchie Snyder to request working full-time on guitar strings. I reviewed the business plan with Ritchie, and he decided to sponsor me in this new role. Good news—being a project person for six months was more stressful than leading a new product launch, and I was thankful to have a real job again.

The guitar strings project was in Flagstaff, Arizona, and I lived in northeast Maryland. I was committing to a lengthy job commute. Flagstaff is beautiful, so I am not complaining. It took me a couple of months to figure out how to manage sleep with a two to three-hour time zone change. Arizona does not have daylight savings time, so the time difference compared to Maryland is two hours in the winter months and three hours in the summer months. It is simple. Do not change time zones. I was asleep by 7 p.m. and woke up at 3 a.m. when visiting Flagstaff. Little America Hotel had a 24-hour gym and restaurant for my early morning activities. My productivity went through the roof with this schedule.

I am naïve with company politics. Is this a weakness or a strength? After committing to guitar strings, I had breakfast with Medical Products leadership, and they offered me a job. I was grateful for the unspecified opportunity but declined. Little did I know that I had made a new adversary in Gore's leadership by declining the job. Oh well, take a number and stand in line. This leader had a reputation for surrounding himself with weak people dependent on him for all decisions, and I am thankful I did not work for him. I struggle to follow a person blindly. I ask questions when appropriate, and I want a voice in decisions. I am loyal to leaders but don't ascribe to blind loyalty. If I were more skilled at managing up, I would have moved to Flagstaff and been a loyal lieutenant working on medical devices. I am joking. I would not pull this off for longer than two weeks.

Guitar String Performance and the Team

I had two challenges with the prototype guitar string performance. First, the coated strings sounded good but not great. Only "good" means not good enough to launch. The second issue was the durability of the coating. It would flake and appear fuzzy after a few hours of use. The shaggy look did not seem to affect the sound, but it looked strange and was distracting. I will rely on my U.S. Navy experience, and it was "All hands on deck" to build an improved coated guitar string that sounded great.

I needed an exceptional technology and manufacturing team if we had any chance of overcoming the product obstacles. Dave recruited Glenn Bethke, Chuck Hebestreit, and Joe Huppenthal for technology and manufacturing innovation. Remarkably, all these associates worked on guitar strings in addition to their day job. Like GLIDE Floss, ask for and graciously accept help from talented people. Unfortunately, our budget was limited, and we begged, stole, and borrowed talent.

Glenn is an expert engineer in fluoropolymers and film technology. He has forgotten more than most people know about films. Glenn is innovative, creative, and focused on adding value, and is one of the three inventors in the ELIXIR Strings patent. Chuck Hebestreit was an exceptional technician and an excellent guitar player. Chuck understood acoustic and electric guitars, and he had an excellent feel for what motivates most guitar players. Chuck spent countless hours evaluating guitar string sound and durability. Joe is the best process engineer and manufacturing leader that I have met in my life. Quiet and unassuming, but scary smart. Joe can be soft-spoken, but you would be wise to stop and listen closely anytime he has something to say.

I was plotting how to recruit Jeannie Guthrie to be a leader in the guitar strings team project. If you want to succeed, work with smart people who have excellent judgment. I valued her financial insight and willingness to engage in manufacturing projects, marketing planning and execution, and sales. Jeannie was also a mentor to many people on the team. Team members felt comfortable reaching out to her to discuss their careers, opportunities, or concerns.

I also convinced Jane Gardner to join our team to lead sales and marketing activities. Jane was returning to Gore from maternity leave, and it was a natural time for her to transition from GLIDE Floss to the guitar strings project. Jane was willing to do any job to make guitar strings a success. David Johns, our intellectual property attorney, would continue to work with us on technology, inventions, patent claims, and branding. David is always excited about new ideas, products, and innovations.

Joe Huppenthal recruited Patti Prescott and Ann Stump, experienced manufacturing associates, to join our team full-time. Patti and Ann worked tirelessly to manufacture prototype strings, establish written processes, and engage with engineers in process automation and quality.

Many people like to talk about the importance of teams. I do not doubt that ELIXIR Strings succeeded because of the individual and collective efforts of a group of intelligent, dedicated, and loyal team members. We were a winning team.

Alpha Test and Beta Test # 1

I began networking with guitar players early in the project. I did not go "Hollywood" and engage with big-name entertainers or bands. Instead, I traveled to music festivals and smaller guitar events and networked with exceptional singer-songwriters and fingerstyle acoustic guitar musicians. I enjoyed meeting dental professionals in my GLIDE Floss days. But musicians are more entertaining. Sorry, I still loved being with dentists and hygienists. Talented guitar players across the country guided me on how best to communicate with other musicians, create a cost-effective guitar string testing protocol, optimize future sampling programs, and build an artist relations program. Several musicians became highly valued ongoing consultants for our team.

Focus is critical in a new product launch. The team must complete thousands of tasks in the proper order. I remember visiting a Gore plant in Germany that I worked with to launch GLIDE Floss in Europe. I do my best to let people do their jobs and manage my inclination to micro-manage. The purpose of my visit was to meet new members of the team and to review progress on our regional business plan. Unfortunately, several months before our meeting, the group decided their first step was to build a packaging and logistics capability to deliver GLIDE Floss to thousands of customers a day. The only problem was we had no orders to ship. In this instance, I behaved myself. Rather than being critical of the logistics capability, I complimented the team on their efforts and let them know they had developed logistics practices to help other sales locations. We spent the rest of our time that week on building a grassroots marketing strategy that would result in orders from dental professionals and retailers. Priorities can be subjective. I worry about getting orders before you make significant investments in a high-volume capability to ship orders. I think the local team was excited to accomplish something, and building a logistics capability is tangible. Building a grassroots marketing plan is filled with uncertainty.

Acoustic guitars have the most significant need for improved consistent sound and long life. Do not get me wrong. There is value in coating electric guitar strings, but the musician has many options to adjust the sound with electronics.

New acoustic guitar strings are a mixed blessing to an accomplished musician. New guitar strings are much brighter than used strings. But most experienced guitar players consider new strings to be too bright. Guitar strings have the preferred sound after three to five hours of play. But guitar strings then gradually decline in tone due to contaminants in the windings and metal corrosion. We set our sights on targeting the sound of a guitar string played for three to five hours and then maintaining this sound. Our coating on the wound guitar string eliminates contamination and reduces corrosion that causes a gradual decline in sound quality. Our value proposition is sound quality that lasts.

The team improved the original "High School Strings" during the next month, including changes to the coating material and the manufacturing process. I organized a test with thirty experienced musicians in Arizona to test the strings. I referred to this as an alpha test. The test's only purpose was to assess the sound quality and life. The musicians used the guitar strings for four weeks. The good news is the musicians believed the coating extended the guitar string's musical life. The bad news is the improved strings sounded good but still not great, and the coating was not durable. In addition, the strings looked fuzzy after ten hours of play.

Over the next few months, Dave, Glenn, and Joe made improvements to the coating and manufacturing process, and the strings were brighter. It was time to get feedback from a much broader group of musicians. I referred to this test as Beta 1. Sound is subjective, and I was anxious to get feedback from thousands of musicians. I guessed that if 50% of the musicians in the test liked our strings' tone and musical life, we had a winning product. For the Beta 1 test, I sent 5,000 sets of guitar strings to subscribers of leading guitar player magazines. I made up the number 5,000. I had three reasons for this number of evaluators. First, it is compelling if 50% of 5,000 musicians preferred our strings. The perception is thousands of musicians' opinions are significant for internal selling. Second, our manufacturing team needed practice making strings and experience to automate the process. Third, 5,000 evaluators would start a grassroots buzz with other musicians. I limited the trial to acoustic guitar because this was the most challenging product to make.

The results of the Beta 1 test was terrible. About 10% of the musicians loved the string. I have learned that 10% of the population loves anything, and you must be careful of these people. If we relied on this 10% of musicians, we would fail. Most musicians confirmed three issues with the Beta 1 product. First, the string sound was bright but not bright enough. The relatively dull sound reinforced the assumption that coating a string dampens the sound. Second, the durability of the coating continued to be unacceptable. And third, the wound strings were ugly with a dirty white and gray appearance. Conventional acoustic guitar strings are a bright gold or brass color. The color did not affect the sound, but who wants an ugly string? The good news is that Dave fixed the appearance while we were conducting the first beta test.

Beta 2 Test – Should We Quit?

It is too easy to quit. Our team had enough data after the Beta 1 test to stop the project and accept that a coated guitar string cannot work. Not one person on the team suggested we quit. We believed in the product and our ability to fix the problems.

I led a weekly team meeting focused on manufacturing and film improvements. My contribution was to take notes and monitor our progress to schedule a new beta test.

It is not a surprise, but the string quality improved as our manufacturing experience grew. Glenn continued to tweak the film for improved sound. Joe worked on different process techniques to improve sound and durability. Chuck worked with a local musician to test the brightness of new string samples. We had planned to use sound level meters and frequency analyzers to test the tone of a coated string versus an uncoated string. At this stage of the project, we found that a musician's ear is better than machines in assessing guitar string tone and brightness.

After two months, we were planning a second beta test. We again sent the strings to 5,000 musicians who were subscribers of leading guitar magazines. Sampling musicians is not as easy as renting a subscriber's name from a magazine and sending the musician strings for testing. Sampling requires a two-step process. Step 1 is a letter to the musician explaining the test with a postage-paid postcard to sign up for the evaluation. Musicians need to specify the string gauge they use on their acoustic guitar. We offered three gauges at the time—Extra Light (.010 to .047), Light (.012 to .053), and Medium (.013 to .056). Guitar players are fussy about the gauge of strings they play. We sent letters to about 10,000 musicians to get 5,000 replies.

We had now been hard at work for fifteen months when we began the Beta 2 test. Leadership is supportive but anxious for a product launch. I had first guessed, I mean estimated, we would need fifteen months for a product launch.

We were late. The team needed the Beta 2 test to be successful.

The Beta 2 test bombed. The sound was better than the Beta 1 product, but less than 50% of the musicians liked the sound. It was still not bright enough for most musicians returning evaluation forms. Coating durability was better, but musicians were distracted by a slightly fuzzy string. We were proving time and again that making a great-sounding, durable coated guitar string is complicated.

I am impressed with the number of musicians who returned their string evaluation in a postage-paid envelope. Selling a consumer product can also be challenging since some consumers are crazy. When you mail a postage-paid postcard, some people will return it with ugly messages. I always included a sample of GLIDE Floss with our experimental guitar strings. It is a great product, and why not give the musician the gift of good oral health. One musician used his postage-paid guitar strings postcard to claim we offered lousy guitar strings to sell GLIDE Floss. Really? Also, be aware of Internet trolls. These people are scum and only take joy in spreading misinformation. A special thank you and shoutout to endorsed musicians like El McMeen (elmcmeen.com), who corrected many falsehoods spread on the Internet.

Beta 3 Test – Inspiration

The clock is ticking.

The team would not accept failure. Work continued, and a successful Beta 3 product was the priority. Joe Huppenthal developed significant innovations in the manufacturing process that "fixed" the Beta 2 string. Joe is a calm and deliberate person. In our weekly meetings, Joe casually commented on developing process changes that improved the string sound and durability. Dave had built a "Pick-O-Matic" to test durability. The Pick-O-Matic plucked a string with a pick, measured the number of plucks, and a technician would score durability based on coating wear at different pick intervals. The local musician listening to test strings reported Joe's latest manufacturing process innovation resulted in the preferred brighter sound. As mentioned, Dave had already fixed the Beta 1 color issues.

Our Beta 3 test with over 5,000 musicians was a big success. Over 50% of musicians liked the sound of the strings. Durability was not an issue. The wound strings would be a little fuzzy after extended play, but this did not affect the sound and was not distracting.

We are in business. A coated guitar string that delivers sound quality that lasts is a big deal. Our team had been hard at work for over eighteen months. We believed in the product, and we trusted each other to do our best to overcome obstacles. The Gore company and Ritchie Snyder deserve credit for patience. Gore values technology, demands product excellence, and will be patient for results if you give them a reason. I discuss innovation in Part 2, Lesson 1. Ritchie was a gifted leader who knew how to protect a team trying to innovate and create a new product. He had high expectations for communication and delivering success, and he rewarded his teams with independence and time. Not many leaders pull this off in any company.

I will make a plug for two exceptional guitar players. Larry Pattis and Pete Huttlinger are the only two musicians I know who participated in all three beta tests. Larry Pattis (larrypattis.com) is a gifted musician and songwriter. He understands the importance of a melody in his songwriting, whether a ballad or an up-tempo song. Larry provided detailed comments on Beta 1 and 2 products. Larry is not shy, and you do not have to wonder what he is thinking. Larry called me after trying Beta 3 strings with a request. Could we send another set of strings for him to record his album? Larry's *Random Chance* album is the first album recorded with ELIXIR Strings, and it is a jewel. You need to check out Larry's music. It is beautiful.

Pete Huttlinger (petehuttlinger.com) is a highly respected Nashville professional guitar player and songwriter. In 1994, Pete joined John Denver's band as lead guitarist until John died in 1997. Pete also played on John Denver's records, and I enjoy watching Pete perform on John Denver's *Wildlife Concert* DVD. Sadly, Pete died in 2016. He was only fifty-four years old, and his positive attitude in dealing with health challenges is an inspiring story. I first met with Pete at the 1996 NAMM trade show in Nashville, and he spent an hour or so with me to provide detailed input on the beta strings. NAMM stands for the National Association of Music Merchants, and they sponsored two trade shows per year dedicated to music products. In my last meeting with Pete, he was excited about the sound and quality of Beta 3 strings. Check out Pete's website listed above and order his music and the book he wrote with Erin Morris Huttlinger, his wife, titled *Joined At The Heart.* You will not be disappointed.

Larry Pattis and Pete Huttlinger were the first ELIXIR Strings endorsed artists.

The Brand

In March 1996, our guitar strings were labeled "Gore Experimental Guitar Strings," packaged in a plastic envelope. Beta testing is underway, and we needed a product brand and new packaging for the launch. Not having a brand during testing of our Beta 1 and 2 strings was a mixed blessing. The "experimental" name allowed the team to make changes at will and did not compromise the ultimate brand.

Most businesses will engage a marketing company specializing in branding to develop a product name and logo, and there are great marketing companies that focus on new product branding. This process is expensive, with six figures being a starting point. I am cheap, and spending money in a business startup is all about choices. If I spend $100,000-plus for a brand and logo, I do not have $100,000 to spend on sampling strings to musicians and creating demand for the product.

Bob Gore came up with the GLIDE brand for dental floss. It is a great brand because it is suggestive and memorable. A brand can be suggestive, but it cannot be descriptive if you want a registered trademark. There is a fine line between suggestive and descriptive. During a guitar strings business review, Bob Gore mentioned that he would approve the guitar strings brand. Bob was exceptional at marketing, so I embraced this request.

Our core team began brainstorming a brand name for our guitar strings and a component brand name for the coating in March 1996. I like component brands because it offers the option to apply our coating technology to other companies' guitar strings. Also, I wanted to focus on the unique coating in our grassroots marketing strategy. Our core team met with our attorney, David Johns, weekly on a Wednesday afternoon in the Medical West plant conference room to brainstorm brand ideas. Each of us arrived at the meeting with a dictionary and a thesaurus. It was generally a green-light meeting. Every idea is a good idea when first suggested. At the end of the session, we would decide that some of the names were not exciting and discarded as a team. Coming up with a good brand is hard work, but it is even more challenging to develop a suggestive brand that is not already trademarked. One early suggestion of a brand that I liked is Sonic Guitar Strings. Sorry, Sonic is not available.

By December 1996, David Johns and his paralegal team had reviewed and disqualified more than 300 possible brand names for guitar strings and the coating component brand. The team was preparing for the final beta test, and the need for a brand name had become critical.

Bob Gore invented expanded PTFE, and the guitar string film is a version of Bob's invention. In December, the team brainstormed component brands when Chuck Hebestreit suggested "BOB's MAGIC ELIXIR" as a component brand. I think Chuck was joking around with this name, but it had a certain ring. Someone in the team observed that "ELIXIR" might be a candidate for the guitar string brand. We became more excited when we looked up the definition of ELIXIR. In medieval times, it was a medicine that extended life. The value of our guitar strings is sound quality that lasts. The team did not immediately embrace the name, but by January 1997, it was our choice. Also, Gore would trademark the ELIXIR brand globally based on a search of the directory of U.S. trademarks. The team also came up with a suggestive coating name. A photomicrograph showed the coating appeared to be a web that encapsulates the wound guitar string. Web became a candidate for the coating name. We came up with POLYWEB® as our coating name, and "poly" comes from polytetrafluoroethylene.

Our brand proposal to Bob Gore was *ELIXIR Guitar Strings featuring POLYWEB Coating.*

On Friday, January 10, 1997, I sent a voice message to Bob Gore with the team's proposal. Within hours, Bob returned the voice message with his approval. I relayed the message to the team. It is a big deal to spend almost ten months in weekly meetings and develop a compelling brand. Mission accomplished.

Bad news. On Monday, January 12, I receive a voice message from Bob Gore. He is concerned with the ELIXIR brand. Bob was at a social event the previous Friday evening and talked with a surgeon who happened to play guitar. Bob mentioned our project and the ELIXIR brand to the doctor. The doctor's response was not good. He suggested to Bob that the name ELIXIR was not consistent with the Gore technology reputation since it evoked an image of cough syrup. Everyone has an opinion. In his message, Bob asked me to send him a summary of our branding discussions.

I am a notetaker, and I had documented the 300-plus names summarized alphabetically in a double-column format. I sent the summary to Bob in an email. The list was impressive when you looked at the range of brands explored by the team. As you can imagine, I was once again nervous about our path forward. Bob reviewed the summary of possible names and responded later in the day that he was good with the ELIXIR brand.

You never really know whether the customer likes a brand until you commit to it. Musicians and music retailers immediately embraced the name ELIXIR. It is memorable. Do you want a good team-play exercise? Work together with a small team for ten months to develop a great brand name.

I worked with Graymatter, a terrific marketing and advertising firm in Phoenix, Arizona. Graymatter does it all, including logo design, advertising, website, and media design, copywriting—you name it. Richard Kronick of Graymatter came up with the tag "See Something You Have Never Heard" for our first coated guitar strings advertisement. With a tight budget, Graymatter came up with an ELIXIR logo and gold-foil packaging that screamed, "I am expensive and worth every penny." I used Graymatter for all our advertising needs with ELIXIR Strings. The logo was updated a few years after I left the team by a different agency, and I like it. Logo updates are good if managed strategically. The packaging color scheme identifying string type was not changed, which is good, and the new logo is distinctive. I suggest you develop a tight relationship with your creative agency. Do not shop your business for every project. It takes too long for the creative agency to know you and understand expectations. You have better ways to spend your time, such as selling products. Graymatter is the best, and I am grateful for its innovation and messaging capability.

Manufacturing Excellence

Manufacturing a coated guitar string with consistent sound is tricky. By comparison, GLIDE Floss manufacturing was relatively easy. Gore was the expert in making fiber for GLIDE Floss. I had the good fortune to connect with Gudebrod, Inc. for dental floss manufacturing, including applying wax, making bobbins, packaging, and logistics. It is not easy making dental floss, but it was easier than making a coated guitar string.

From the beginning, Joe Huppenthal, Patti Prescott, Ann Stump, and Jeannie Guthrie had a vision for manufacturing quality and efficiency. Automation, when feasible, was a priority from the start. Most people hear the word automation and figure it is all about lowering costs. For guitar strings, automation results in higher quality, consistent sound, and reduced costs. Dependable guitar string sound and durability demand consistency in materials and processes.

I have experience in manufacturing and automation from my time in the Gore Polymer Products Team. I also have the good judgment to step aside and watch Joe, Patti, Ann, and Jeannie do their magic as the team invested in additional manufacturing capacity to meet expected demand. Joe recruited Janet Khamashta to our team. Janet is an experienced and skillful manufacturing and process design engineer. We were lucky to have Janet on our team, and she became the driving force for automation and matching capacity to increasing demand. The team was cost-conscious and provided regular updates to the broader team. Janet worked closely with Jeannie Guthrie to forecast capital investments.

Gore manufacturing processes are confidential and proprietary, and I cannot discuss the details of the advanced technology to manufacture a coated guitar string. Take my word for it. The process is complex.

The Launch

The launch of ELIXIR Strings was unconventional. We were in the music marketplace for one and a half years, pushing our experimental strings while launching a grassroots testing campaign. Before the launch, we exhibited at two NAMM Shows, visiting music retailers, attending folk festivals, and sampling thousands of musicians with our Beta 1, 2, and 3 products labeled "Gore Experimental Guitar Strings."

This strategy is risky. Some musicians might be hesitant to support the final product if exposed to an inferior performing Beta 1 and Beta 2 product. However, the benefits proved to outweigh the risks. You learn from listening to people, making minor mistakes, and learning how to best spend a limited grassroots marketing budget. By the time we launched a commercial product, most industry experts and leading musicians knew who we were, and I had a credible launch plan.

Earlier, I mentioned Graymatter and my favorite ad of all time. Graymatter developed a print advertisement placed in *Acoustic Guitar* magazine inviting retailers to our booth at the January 1997 NAMM trade show. It featured a Beta 3 string photomicrograph on a soft blue background with the simple tag "See Something You've Never Heard Before." The ad included our booth number. The picture of the coated string in the ad became a part of our brand messaging. The image appears as a milky-white transparent web surrounding a gold wound guitar string. This ad created a buzz and drove music store owners to our booth.

ELIXIR Strings was officially launched at our third NAMM trade show in Nashville from July 11 to 13, 1997. Finally.

Have you been interviewed and then quoted in a print article? I have found my quotes to be close, but not exactly what I said. I remember one print article claiming I came up with the GLIDE Floss brand. It is nice, but I never took credit for Bob Gore's brand. People's versions of history can change over time. In 2006, I attended a presentation by the ELIXIR Strings team that included a slide detailing the product launch at our third NAMM trade show. The presentation claimed music store retailers immediately embraced the product, and we were an instant hit. Product orders exceeded expectations.

I did not remember this version of events. Our team had a different problem at this trade show, specifically, price shock, and did not write many orders.

A set of acoustic guitar strings goes for $3 in the store. The wholesale price is $1.50 per set, with ten sets per box, $15 per box. ELIXIR Strings suggested retail price was $15 per set. Our price was five times the price of a conventional set of guitar strings. The wholesale price was $7.50, 10 sets per box, $75 per box. Store owners thought I was an idiot and confused the suggested retail price per set versus the price per box of ten sets. The $75 per box wholesale price was absurd to most music store owners. Value pricing can be disruptive!

Grassroots Marketing and Sales

Ask anyone whether launching a product is easy. The answer is an emphatic *no* if you have worked in the launch. ELIXIR Strings is a commercial success because we have a great product and did an excellent job integrating sales and marketing with a grassroots focus. But, of course, we had eighteen months from idea to launch to figure this out.

The first challenge is many musicians did not believe a coated string could sound good. Applying a coating must dampen vibration and impact brightness, right? Retail distribution is also challenging. There are only a few chain music retailers and about 4,250 independent stores. In 1997, the Internet helped share information but was relatively new for online sales. For example, Amazon did not begin sales of music CDs until 1998.

The beta test sampling program worked to our advantage and started grassroots word-of-mouth excitement. In GLIDE Floss, sample one dental hygienist, and if excited, the hygienist would tell one hundred patients. Twenty of those patients would listen. Thousands of dental hygienists were influencing hundreds of thousands of patients to buy GLIDE Floss.

There is no one like a dental hygienist in the music industry. Early in the project, I guessed the best way to influence musicians and establish credibility was for guitar manufacturers to install ELIXIR Strings at the factory. Martin Guitars feature Martin strings, and it seems most Martin Guitar owners prefer Martin strings because of the manufacturer association. I was also solving a problem for guitar manufacturers. A new guitar arrives at the retail store with great sound. Now imagine every guitar geek in the county arriving at the retailer to check out the new guitar. Within weeks, the guitar string windings are contaminated, and the great sound is fading. ELIXIR Strings offer sound quality that lasts. The new guitar will sound great for months. You cannot beat this.

Taylor Guitars is my favorite acoustic guitar brand. Bob Taylor is the president and co-founder of Taylor Guitars, and he is an exceptional entrepreneur and leader. A small team from Gore visited Taylor Guitars at their factory in El Cajon, California, to assess their interest in working together. The Taylor Guitars management team was welcoming and gracious. We were naïve, but we were sincere in our belief that ELIXIR Strings had high value. After a plant tour, I made the sales pitch for Taylor Guitars to feature ELIXIR Strings from the factory.

Rather than telling us to get lost, Bob Taylor coached us. It was not a lecture; it was a teaching moment. Bob liked ELIXIR

Strings and personally used them. He explained that he had spent many years building his brand. Bob advised us to keep him apprised of our progress in the market. We would speak again when the ELIXIR brand was a great success with musicians. I agree with Bob Taylor's assessment, and I received similar feedback from other guitar manufacturers.

This news was not good for my grassroots marketing plan, and we needed to regroup. As a side story, I recently decided to take guitar lessons. Larry Pattis (larrypattis.com) helped me select the Taylor 414ce-R model. It is a beautiful guitar, and I only wish it had a more accomplished guitar owner.

So, how did we change gears in our grassroots marketing plan?

I assume that a customer of any new product needs at least three exposures before purchasing the product. The first contact is just a memory. A typical response after one exposure might be, "Yes, I have heard of the product." This response is like the story of the five stages of the career of a musician. I will pretend I am a musician.

Stage 1: Who is John Spencer?

Stage 2: I have heard of John Spencer.

Stage 3: Get me John Spencer.

Stage 4. Get me someone just like John Spencer.

Stage 5. Who is John Spencer?

The foundation of our grassroots plan was targeting thousands of select musicians with samples and feedback forms. My initial focus was (1) musicians who had participated in our beta testing and (2) guitar instructors. Fortunately, I was able to rent the names of subscribers from a magazine focused on guitar instructors. Just like our beta test, the musician received a letter in the mail with a postage-paid reply card for a sample of ELIXIR Guitar Strings. The musician selects their preferred gauge and mails the card to Gore. We send strings with a feedback form. A few months later, we once again offered the musician a sample of ELIXIR Guitar Strings, with a request they ask their local retailer to stock the product. The musician might receive a third set of free strings, and we always requested they ask their local retailer to stock the product.

In parallel, our grassroots marketing plan for the 4,250 music stores includes quarterly mailings and placing quarterly phone calls. And we were out visiting music retailers. We did not visit 4,000 retailers, but we traveled to quite a few. Many store owners were fussy about cold calls, so it was always best to call ahead for an appointment.

How does a small team accomplish this enormous action plan?

First, we contracted with a fulfillment center to package and mail samples to musicians and retailers. The fulfillment center we used specialized in creating job opportunities for disabled people, so this is a win for everyone. Second, mailings to musicians were ongoing, and music store mailings were every three months. The mailing to music stores would include a letter, ELIXIR String catalog, a reprint of a magazine advertisement, and an 800 number to place an order.

Contacting music retailers by telephone was a unique challenge. We needed to reach 4,000-plus retailers two weeks after the quarterly mailing. I was lucky to hook up with a leading catalog retailer specializing in selling food, including Wisconsin cheese, candy, and gift baskets. Their busy time was the Christmas holiday, Valentine's Day, and Thanksgiving. Their expert customer service team was available at other times to make telephone sales calls. We arrived quarterly for training, and they made professional sales calls at a reasonable cost in January, April, June, and early October. The call-center training focused on listening to retailers, answering questions from a script, and always ask for an order! Many people are shy about asking for a purchase order. Not me. Always ask for the order.

People like to talk and see people. As mentioned, members of our team would go on road trips and visit music retailers. To increase the number of music stores we visited, I selectively hired musicians to visit music retailers to demonstrate ELIXIR Strings, answer questions, and ask for an order. The first musician we engaged in this activity was Michael Lille (michaellillemusic.com). Michael was performing at the Kerrville Folk Festival when I met him. He is a talented guitar player, songwriter, and genuinely nice person. We engaged Michael as a contractor to visit music retailers in the Midwest. During one store visit, the retailer commented that he had recently received our quarterly mailing. The store owner answered a telephone call from our outsourced call center while talking with Michael by coincidence. The store owner handed the phone to Michael thinking the call center was trying to reach him. A few months later, Michael joined our team full-time to lead marketing, artist relations, and sales initiatives. He was a brilliant hire. The bottom line is, reaching over 4,000 retailers with a new and disruptive product takes time and effort. It is not easy, so be innovative and seek partners to lower costs.

Another grassroots campaign was sponsorship and attendance at music festivals focused on acoustic music. Our first sponsorship was the Kerrville Folk Festival held at the Quiet Valley Ranch, about an hour's drive from San Antonio in the Texas hill country. If you enjoy music, add the Kerrville Folk Festival to your bucket list. The event was started in 1972 by Rod Kennedy and features acoustic music and songwriters. It is eighteen days and nights of concerts, songwriting workshops, and other entertainment. Did I mention I was lucky? Kerrville had just lost a lead sponsor in 1997, and ELIXIR Strings stepped in to fill the gap. Rod Kennedy and his staff went over the top to promote ELXIR Strings to the musicians performing at the festival and the thousands of attendees at the evening concerts. The word was out that ELIXIR Strings had saved the day with our sponsorship, and we secured exceptional goodwill from musicians. I need to revisit this festival. Our team attended six festivals and guitar events per year, and we networked with professional musicians and amateur guitar players at all skill levels.

Our team would meet with hundreds of music retailers at the NAMM Shows in July and January, and we always sent a special mailing with samples before the shows. Always include a reason for the retailer to visit with you at the booth. Many retailers would comment on a recent mailing, a customer service call, or a store visit. And retailers were placing an order because local guitar players asked them to stock the product. For example, a music store owner placed an order at NAMM, and he was unhappy. The owner did not like our pricing, and if it were up to him, he would not place an order. But "I am just getting too many people asking for the strings." Perfect! Creating demand is grassroots marketing and sales.

Another element of our plan was a limited two-level musician endorsement program featuring the musicians on the elixirstrings.com website, promoting musicians at sponsored music festivals, and limited print advertisement promotion. Our artist relations program expected that the musician would advise people that they endorsed ELIXIR Guitar Strings and feature our logo in concert materials and recordings. Again, our focus was working musicians, not headlining entertainers. These exceptional musicians are loyal and a worthwhile investment.

Also, I scheduled ongoing updates to guitar manufacturers on our launch progress, retail availability, and gauging their interest in installing ELIXIR Strings from the factory with a hangtag. Unfortunately, there was zero interest in the first eighteen months following our launch. But do not give up hope if you have a good idea.

The key to a successful grassroots marketing and sales plan is execution. I have talked with many people leading startups over the years. I am surprised at how many of these leaders will negatively comment on an element of their marketing plan. It's usually something like, "I tried sampling the product, but it did not work. Sales did not grow." The person tried sampling once, and it did not work. There is a joke I like. "I dusted once. It came back. You will not fool me again." You must be persistent and repeat your programs with crisp messaging. Crisp messaging looks easy, but it is not. Early GLIDE Floss promotional materials were impossible to read. I wanted to tell the hygienist or consumer everything I knew. Stop. Tell your customers what they need to know. People receive way too much messaging and communication. I have learned time and again to keep it simple and easily noticed.

During the launch, an important metric was the number of retailers stocking ELIXIR Strings. The more important metric is tracking the reorder rate by product type. Jeannie Guthrie and I estimated we needed a minimum of 500 music retailers selling ELIXIR Guitar Strings with a reorder every two months for our business to be profitable. Our goal was to have 500 retailers stocking products by September 1997.

I was not near 500 stores by September. Also, our reorder rate was not meeting my expectations.

The first six months following our launch was a scary time. Finally, we have a great product. Musician feedback is excellent. The shock of our pricing seemed to be under control. But sales were lagging. I recall having some doubts about the future success of ELIXIR Strings in early 1998. Maybe I screwed up the pricing, and ELIXIR Strings did not have broad appeal at five times the price of conventional strings? Perhaps too many guitar players would not accept that a coated string sounds good? Maybe our integrated sales and marketing plan was not that great?

Be patient.

Being patient is not my strength.

Sales activity finally picked up in late 1997. In January 1998, we achieved our ELIXIR Strings goal of being available in 500 music retailers. By March 1998, ELIXIR Strings were available for sale in nearly 800 retailers. The reorder rate met expectations. Meeting expectations means I wanted a higher reorder rate, but it was acceptable.

In July 1998, Tacoma Guitars became the first guitar manufacturer to outfit new guitars with ELIXIR Strings and a hangtag. In November 1998, ELIXIR Strings received the prestigious "Players Choice Award" from *Acoustic Guitar* magazine. Sales increased!

Great news. In June 1999, Taylor Guitars began outfitting new guitars with ELIXIR Strings. Many guitar manufacturers followed. I count more than eighty guitar manufacturers who use ELIXIR Guitar Strings on the Gore website. Great job!

In July 1999, we achieved our annualized sales objective, and ELIXIR Strings was profitable. It was only two years from our launch, but it felt much longer.

In November 2000, we launched ELXIR Strings featuring NANOWEB® Coating. NANOWEB Coating was the next advance for players who wanted a brighter sound that lasts longer. Again, our team continued to innovate! I love NANOWEB Coating. It is so thin you cannot see it visually, and the guitar sings.

Innovation goes beyond products. Our team was active visiting music retailers, and we needed to view actual sales activity for the 4,250 independent stores. Gore IT systems did not allow for this capability from the field. Jeannie Guthrie and I worked with a Flagstaff IT genius to develop a compelling online sales analysis application. This software developer built a customer relationship management software for ELIXIR Guitar Strings in two weekends of programming. Before a sales call, our team could now research which strings were stocked by the retailer and their reorder rates. Real-time music retailer sales information in 1998 was a massive advance in our sales capability. Our software was an early version of a successful customer relationship management tool.

We drank from a fire hose in 1998 and needed to expand the team.

Carolyn Harrell joined the team in April 1998 as our first dedicated product specialist. A Gore product specialist is like an orchestra's conductor, and the person owns the product and drives functional excellence alignment. Functions include technology, research, manufacturing, sales, marketing, and administrative support. The best product specialists have an extreme passion for their product and the Gore company. Carolyn was a great product specialist and future business leader; she was bright, hardworking, and intense desire to succeed. Sadly, Carolyn passed away in 2001 from a heart attack. She was only forty-three years old. Carolyn's death was a massive blow to me, as her friend, and the ELIXIR Strings team.

Following the commercial launch, Jeannie, Jane, and I recruited expert sales help from the GLIDE Floss team to help us part-time. Janifer Brown was a sales leader for GLIDE Floss and lived in Seattle. Janifer took the lead in engaging with west coast music retailers, and she was exceptionally talented with the onboarding of new salespeople. Janifer is a natural salesperson— honest, personable, and trustworthy.

Many musicians played a significant role in the launch and acceptance of ELIXIR Strings. By early 1998, there were about sixty endorsed musicians. In addition, we hired musicians to visit music retailers, work on NAMM trade shows, and perform at sponsored events. I previously mentioned Pete Huttlinger (petehuttlinger.com), Larry Pattis (larrypattis.com), and Michael Lille (michaellillesongs.com). Other musicians who played a significant role in the launch include Michael Camp (michaelcamp.com), Kate Wallace (katewallace.com), El McMeen (elmcmeen.com), and Brian Doherty from Evans & Doherty (evansanddoherty.com).

ELIXIR Guitar Strings integrated sales and marketing benefited from a rolling twelve-month scheduling calendar. Product launches are a puzzle, and you must work on multiple pieces of the puzzle simultaneously. You will only know if you have an excellent grassroots strategy after the fact. If your plan works, you were brilliant. If you fail, then you did not put together an acceptable plan. Not knowing the future is the fun and scary part. I had more fun from June 1997 to December 1998 than you can imagine. A great product, an exceptional team, and a successful grassroots marketing and sales plan. Can it get any better than this?

Expanded Geography

The United States was the focus of the launch of ELIXIR Strings.

Our team launched ELIXIR Strings in Germany at the February 1998 Music Messe show in Frankfurt, Germany. I had built relationships in Europe with Gore Associates, who would drive new commercial products. One of the challenges was a meager marketing budget that resulted in bad grassroots marketing decisions. Sampling to musicians was tactical, and contact with musicians and regular communication with music stores was hit or miss. Sales were modest—no, sales were terrible. Our Brazil subsidiary also stocked ELIXIR Strings and sold them to music stores by request. No marketing plan or marketing budget. If I could do it again, I would delay international sales until the regional businesses were willing to invest in a limited and focused grassroots marketing and sales plan.

The leading music products distributor in Canada had no use for ELIXIR Strings in the early years. The company believed our product was a fad, and interest would decline with time. However, Brian Doherty of Evans & Doherty (evansanddoherty.com), an endorsed artist, requested to be a distributor in 1998. Why not? In addition to being a talented musician, Brian is an entrepreneur who owns and operates Eastern Entertainment Agency, a booking agency and production company for many Canadian and international acts. In 2000, he opened The Old Triangle Irish Alehouse in Halifax. There are now four restaurant locations, including Halifax, Moncton, Charlottetown, and Sydney. We signed a simple distributor agreement with Brian Doherty, and he sold ELIXIR Strings to music retailers in Canada from his business in Halifax.

I believe that the ELIXIR Strings leadership unfairly fired Brian as a distributor. It is a sad story. Brian had steady sales in Eastern Canada and was an advocate when others in Canada dismissed our product. I contacted the ELIXIR Strings business leader to ask him to reconsider the decision to fire Brian as a distributor, and he abruptly told me to get lost. He may have used an expletive or two when I reached out. The leader, and I use this term loosely, told me exclusivity was a condition of sales to the large Canadian distributor. I do not believe in exclusivity. At the time, ELIXIR Strings' leader was an idiot, which is a reminder that life is not always fair.

A Singapore distributor visited our booth at our launch at the NAMM Show in 1997. Gore did not have a subsidiary in Singapore, and we were free to sign a distributor agreement. The sticking point is sales are limited to Singapore. This distributor sales and reorders were absurdly high for the next three months. You would have thought Singapore was the guitar capital of the world. We learned the distributor was diverting ELIXIR Strings to many countries in Asia-Pacific, including Japan. Unfortunately, we had to end this relationship to honor agreements with Gore subsidiaries. This distributor knew how to sell guitar strings.

I could have done a better job building a more compelling business case in Germany, Brazil, Japan, and Australia to sell the need for marketing investments. Time is your most precious asset, and there is never enough time. Our team worked hard, and I am not sure any of us would have taken the time to focus our attention on global opportunities without compromising our United States launch. I have no regrets.

A Few Misses

Not every marketing or sales initiative worked in the launch of ELIXIR Strings. If you do not have a few misses, you need to experiment more.

In 1998, I released two promotional music CDs featuring endorsed artists. The music CDs were titled *Great Strings Great Music*, and Volume 1 was a twelve-song set that alternated between vocal and instrumental. Volume 2 was a Christmas Holiday collection. I featured the CDs in sales promotions to independent music retailers. The program did not influence sales one way or another, and I discontinued the program. I still enjoy listening to these CDs, and the promotion did give our team another opportunity to talk to music store owners.

I was obsessed with expanding sales to the "casual player" in 1998 and 1999. Casual players own a guitar but do not play it very often. They may not know whether they prefer Extra Light, Light, or Medium strings. A benefit of ELIXIR Strings featuring POLYWEB Coating is that they are easier on the casual player's fingers on the left hand. I developed a single acoustic and electric guitar packaging option with more descriptive text. Casual players may not visit a music retailer, so the plan was to distribute these two SKUs in national and regional chain stores that sold books and electronics. We sold some products, but it was evident in a few months that this product would not work in the long term.

I explored a sales opportunity to purchase inexpensive guitars in bulk, fit them with ELIXIR Strings, and sell the combination on television shopping channels. For only $75, Grandma could buy a guitar featuring ELIXIR Strings for her favorite grandchild. I made several sales calls to the leading shopping channels, but there was no interest. Today, this sounds like a bad idea.

There are many more misses. The point I am making is to experiment. Do not spend a lot of money. If it works, do more of it. If it does not work, stop. The ELIXIR String misses were so small, no one noticed.

Time to Move On

ELIXIR Strings' successful launch looks easy in hindsight, but it was tough. A fantastic team of people came together to overcome product performance issues, build an efficient manufacturing platform, and execute an integrated grassroots marketing and sales plan. As a result, we disrupted the music business with a product that was five times the price of conventional guitar strings. Bill Gore founded the Gore company to "make money and have fun." ELIXIR Strings met this mission statement, and this startup was a blast.

In July 2000, I worked at the NAMM Show, and Ritchie Snyder attended the event. The ELIXIR Strings booth was bustling, and the business was delivering sustainable sales with good margins. While walking the show, Ritchie suggested a new position for me in Gore. Ritchie told me I was good at driving product development, building a launch plan, and delivering a successful business with growing sales and healthy margins. As a result, I am officially labeled "a startup guy."

Ritchie suggested I lead a new business venture in our Fabrics Division to manufacture and sell GORE-TEX and WINDSTOPPER® apparel. The Fabrics Division's traditional model was to sell fabric to outerwear companies. I would create a new forward integration business model that would be disruptive and highly profitable. I was intrigued by this unique job opportunity, and I enjoy disrupting and challenging jobs. I made a pitch to Jeannie Guthrie to join me to lead this effort, and she agreed. ELIXIR Strings was in good hands with Carolyn Harrell taking on business leadership responsibilities.

It seemed like the right time to move on, and I was excited! I enjoy new challenges. Who would figure this new job would be a train wreck?

But that is another story.

Part 2:
Six Lessons in Launching New Products

A fresh look at six lessons learned in launching
new products and how you can improve your
chances of achieving grassroots business
success.

Lesson 1. The Product

An Easy Lesson

Lesson 1—the product is everything.

Nothing else matters if your customer does not value your offering. Forget business plans, pricing, grassroots marketing, sales, building a team, and financial goals if your product does not perform as promised.

I am old school and believe Dr. W. Edwards Demming had it right. From the beginning, you must engineer quality in your product to create customer loyalty. You must be objective, which can be challenging when the product is not cooperating. As mentioned, the customer, not you, decides if you have a valuable product.

The product is your child, and you have the responsibility to develop this toddler.

The Idea

Every product begins with an idea. I wish I had a dime for every product idea that never became a successful product. I would have lots of dimes. I define a successful new product as making a reasonable profit. Product launches are a marathon, not a sprint. It takes me three to five years to come up with an idea, develop the product, build manufacturing capability, launch, and achieve product success.

I have witnessed product champions discuss a product idea as if it were a commercial product. GLIDE Floss was an idea on a chalkboard in Ritchie Snyder's office, and it had been an idea for over twenty years. The preferred fiber denier was uncertain, and the best method to improve floss grip was undecided. Fiber width control and fibrillation were a challenge, and a floss dispenser did not exist. Dave Myers had the idea of an improved coated guitar string. Dave and other expert engineers and scientists worked for two years to make the string sound great and confirm long-lasting musical life.

I enjoy brainstorming product ideas and find there is no shortage of new product concepts. It is exhilarating to commit to transforming an idea into a valuable product. All things are possible when your new product is just an idea.

Innovation

Ideas are the beginning of innovation, and most ideas solve a problem. Conventional dental floss shreds and snaps into gums. Traditional guitar strings sound great for a short time before contamination and corrosion progressively destroy the guitar's tone. GLIDE Floss and ELIXIR Strings solved these problems. Innovation can be as simple as affixing a functional key ring or digital-friendly pocket in the design of a jacket.

Innovation requires a culture of disruption, unconventional thinking, and freedom to fail.

A culture of creativity is a tall task, even in an entrepreneurial and technology company like Gore. Everyone likes innovation, but corporate bureaucracy, lousy managers, and personalities destroy new ideas and creativity. Dave Myers is the most creative person I know. I recently discussed idea generation with Dave, and he gave me a good observation of poor managers he has encountered. "Managers have control when they say no, and there is no power in the word yes." Managers tend to destroy innovation. Leaders have the responsibility to energize innovation. Celebrate the problem-solver and protect the person from the organization.

Product innovation never ends. ELIXIR Strings is a great product, but there were several times it would have been easy to quit, with words like "We gave it our all." But the team never stopped innovating. Improvements in film technology and the manufacturing process by talented engineers and scientists resulted in a guitar string with consistent bright sound with extended musical life. I noticed from elixirstrings.com that Gore offers phosphor bronze acoustic strings, 80/20 bronze acoustic strings, and a new electric guitar string featuring OPTIWEB® coating. Wow. Hats off to the current ELIXIR Strings team for continued innovation.

GLIDE Floss was not a piece of cake. Fiber technology had been around for twenty years. Still, no one had developed a fiber specification for a preferred dental floss, a light wax coating for grip, and an innovative dispenser that dental hygienists and consumers would purchase. I am proud of Patent US5518012A—Expanded PTFE floss material and method of making same—that I worked on with two exceptional engineers, John Dolan and Ray Minor. I had settled on an 1150 denier fiber after testing denier preference from 800 to 1250 denier with people who floss. Still, the fiber's width was controlled by folding before the spooling process. As a result, the width varied, and at times, the fold looked shabby. There was another challenge. The fibers team believed the thin edges of the fiber resulted in fibrillation.

Fibrillation is different than shredding. Dental floss shredding happens when floss breaks off between teeth, whereas fibrillation is the fiber's splitting to form separate continuous fibers. The fiber folding before spooling also increased the floss's thickness, and inconsistencies might impact optimal cleaning. It was rare, but the fiber could unfold during use. The invention resulted in an expanded PTFE dental floss with uniform dimensions. Perfecting the manufacture of fiber for dental floss is innovation, and we did not fall into the trap of "good enough." We launched GLIDE Floss with a folded fiber and transitioned to a superior fiber about one year later.

I worked on a failed project I call "The Barn Coat" that is all about innovation, with the ultimate challenge to (1) create an active lifestyle technology apparel collection and (2) reinvent an established outerwear value chain. Our first task was to create a small lifestyle apparel collection, and we had several terrific designs. The GORE-TEX Classic Jacket for men and women was relatively simple and weighed just a little more than an apple, with an adjustable hood. I liked the versatile GORE-TEX Sierra Jacket design for women. Design features included five pockets, side gussets for a comfortable fit, a gusset key pocket, underarm zippers, and a foldaway adjustable hood. It was great for day hiking, walking, cycling, or work for $199. A less expensive alternative was the Women's GORE-TEX Santa Fe jacket featuring an asymmetric front zipper and "digital friendly" inside pockets for $149. It was our first collection, and we did have a couple of misses. For example, people like the idea of a 3-in-1 jacket, but not the reality. A 3-in-1 jacket is (1) a GORE-TEX shell jacket with a fleece lining for cold weather, (2) a removable liner leaving just a shell jacket, and (3) the liner as a fleece jacket. Sounds good, but not a winner. It was just too much trouble to unzip and zip liners. Always dream with your eyes wide open.

It is difficult to predict success when an innovator comes up with an idea. Leadership would have laughed at me if I had forecasted actual sales of GLIDE Floss. Dave Myers did not know if ELIXIR Strings would be a success when he first had the idea of a better guitar string. I had high hopes for a GORE-TEX and WINDSTOPPER lifestyle apparel collection. This project failed, and I think about this lost opportunity nearly every day. If you are in a launch team, be optimistic and work hard every day to achieve success. Attitude is critical in the launch of a new product.

One lesson carved in stone is never innovate with a customer. Never! You ask for trouble because no one will remember who came up with a good idea. If you and your customer co-own the intellectual property, you will likely have difficulty expanding the use beyond the single customer co-owner. What if the customer sells their rights to the IP? Talk with customers about their problems and preferences, and then return to your offices, labs, and shops to work on solutions.

I like a robust product development funnel. There was no shortage of consumer product ideas at Gore, and I listed every concept as they happened. Many ideas did not proceed far in product development because the technology was outside Gore's experience, or the idea was not superior to alternatives. Some ideas deserved to have been developed into successful products but did not have leadership support. There is never enough money to do everything, and new project investments must be prioritized. Sometimes the answer is, "No."

Passion for your new idea is required unless it negatively impacts your judgment. Personal bias can happen when you are the customer of your product. There is a tendency to set specifications to suit your personal preferences. I do not like GLIDE Floss, and I did not play guitar when I worked on ELIXIR Strings. I listened more closely to hygienists and musicians during the development of floss and guitar strings. I love GORE-TEX and WINDSTOPPER apparel, and it is a superior technology. It is tough to admit, but my personal preferences biased garment styles, colors, and even sizing in "The Barn Coat" story. A person is more likely to innovate when they have an open mind. The apparel collection might have been different and better if I were not such a fan of GORE-TEX and WINDSTOPPER fabric technology.

Innovation must go far beyond new products in a launch. I contributed to and witnessed exceptional advances in manufacturing efficiencies over the years. Marketing offers limitless opportunities to experiment with new ideas and assess the impact on sales. My most innovative idea was my proposal for Gore to sell GLIDE Floss, a branded consumer product, in drugstores, grocery stores, and to mass merchants with a grassroots marketing and sales model. The conventional model at Gore was to sell a component fiber product to a consumer products company. Five years later, Gore leadership had no concern about launching a branded guitar string in retail.

One challenge in a new launch is job security and recognition for the early innovators of the new product. How many startup team members who develop and launch a product are with the business five years later? I have never seen a study, but my opinion is not many. Managers arrive when they see a profitable new business and take over. Removing the innovators from a successful team after three to five years of uncertainty and hard work must be accomplished with sensitivity and proper reward for the startup's success. Jeannie Guthrie and I had moved on from ELIXIR Strings to work in the Fabrics Division. Leadership showed up and announced a move of ELIXIR Strings manufacturing from Flagstaff to the east coast, and the team that created the business was assigned new jobs. It seemed to me that management was satisfied that startup team members did not lose their jobs. Were the new jobs enjoyable, fulfilling, and with the same responsibility? It is just my opinion, but the assigned jobs were not as exciting. I believe moving the guitar strings product manufacturing was the correct business decision. Still, leaders were not sensitive to the people who had given their heart and soul to build ELIXIR Strings, and the change was demoralizing to the innovators.

The following is my Top 10 list that limits innovation in a company:

1. Managers versus Leaders. Managers prefer to manage, not lead, and my experience is that managers are the #1 reason for low morale and lack of innovation in an organization. The worst managers believe they are the most intelligent person in the room, and the organization needs their brilliance to make the tough calls. Incremental change is standard and then positioned as creative thinking. Managers have power, and they will not likely receive substantive feedback that they are destroying innovation. Inspirational leaders embrace innovation and protect the innovators from corporate bureaucracy and the challenges of the status quo.

2. Organizational Resistance. Most people do not like change, and innovation can disrupt the status quo in a business. Status quo is a particular challenge in (1) existing businesses and (2) shortly after a new product achieves success. The innovator is perceived as too disruptive and positioned as a poor team player. Have you heard the line, "This is the way we do things"? The way we do things is organizational resistance.

3. Protecting Existing Business. Most managers and team members are more worried about protecting existing sales and business models than growing new sales, which can be true even when sales are declining. A dying business not committed to change demonstrates absolute loyalty to the status quo. I have attended thousands of monthly business reviews over the years. It frustrates me that a monthly discussion of inventory receives much more attention than new products and ideas. If innovation is not a consistent agenda item in ongoing business reviews, it is not a priority. Leadership can be more loyal to the existing business.

4. Embracing Process Over Results. I am a fan of project tools that help you focus and go faster. Unfortunately, some project tools or business reviews can be barriers to progress by requiring absurd activity to proceed to the next "gate" or "horizon event." The process begins to wag the tail, rather than product development and testing, manufacturing, and building a grassroots marketing and sales plan. Years ago, I was required to use a new project tool that required answering questions about whether a product was "real" before making enough prototypes to understand challenges. It took almost eighteen months to make ELIXIR Strings "real," and this fantastic product may not have proceeded beyond an alpha test using this lousy project tool. The tool also required early calculations of whether the new product was "worth it." In the first weeks of a project, estimates of volume, pricing, distribution, and margins are wild guesses. This tool encouraged gaming financial assumptions to get permission to go to the next phase of the project. My experience is lousy managers embrace ineffective project tools.

5.   **Punishing Risk-Taking.** Innovation and new ideas are risky and may fail. The key to failure is objectivity and learning to improve the odds of success in the next venture. Was the product flawed, pricing too high, grassroots marketing plan ineffective, or the business model just too disruptive for the organization? I failed in selling an overly disruptive business model in an established business after eighteen months of hard work. The result was being humiliated in front of my peers and my manager's broad communication that I would never lead another product startup in the company. My big mistake or failure was communicating but not "connecting" with the leadership on the level of disruption. Eventually, I moved on to innovate in another company. How many people will take a risk in this environment?

6. Lack of Recognition of Innovators. Innovators may not receive the credit or positive attention they deserve. My experience is the better path in a corporate career, especially salary growth, is to manage an existing business than leading a new product launch. Even worse, managers of existing businesses show up like vultures to take over a new business once it is profitable and the innovator is left looking for work. Being an innovator can be a challenging career. I was labeled "a startup guy" and "Mr. Product Introduction." It sounds like a compliment but being a startup guy means you never enjoy your new business's success and ensure that it continues to innovate.

7. Fear of Failure or Making a Mistake. Not everyone enjoys ambiguity and the unknown of launching a new product and business. Launching an innovative product sounds fun but can quickly be overwhelming. For example, committing to your first sales forecast of a product and placing orders for materials and manufacturing equipment can be highly stressful. What if I make a mistake? I have watched projects take years to fail by slow-walking activity to be sure there are no mistakes. Then, of course, the project fails due to the error in slow-walking an action plan. Innovators must be willing to go fast and make small mistakes and learn from them.

8. Poor Execution. An excellent strategy for a new product will fail if you are not good at project execution. Most people do not want to admit poor execution, so the product, customer, or market are blamed. Some innovators are not good at managing details in launching a new product but consistently develop new product ideas. The solution is to team up these innovators with process-focused people.

9.   Low Morale and No Time to Innovate. If you are in a hostile work environment, innovation will suffer. Many team members will feel that nobody cares. Have you ever been in a job where daily responsibilities take more than 100% of your time? I have, and innovation stops in this environment. The goal becomes daily survival.

10.   Innovators Are Not Trained to Sell Ideas. Successful innovators must sell their ideas internally and consistently reinforce the sales message for continued support by leadership. Innovators wrongly assume smart people will embrace new ideas and disruption. Many innovators are naïve and wrongly assume managers will be there to back them up. Training innovators on how to sell internal projects is a worthy investment.

Honorable mentions for innovation killers include micromanagement, suggestion boxes, limiting technology options, narrow business and technology models, too many experts who know better, fear of the unknown, and low operational agility.

It is much easier to kill innovation than to inspire innovation.

The solution to these ten challenges is inspirational leadership described in Lesson 5 – Leadership and Teams.

Product Value Statements

Bob Gore, the Gore company Chairman and CEO, was the master of clear, crisp product value statements.[1] Bob was customer-focused, and he wanted product descriptions to emphasize customer benefits. I think this obsession with the product, as championed by Bob, explains much of the Gore company's success.

It is not easy to write a product value statement early in a project. Gore is a technology company and focused on selling unique products. To establish "unique," Associates were encouraged to use the word "the only." I overthink this word because any new product competes with alternatives and copycats within a year or two. It is incredible how quickly people can copy an idea and develop a creative workaround for a patent.

I think the most compelling product value statements are under ten words, and you might have a page of footnotes to describe what a word means. So, for me, marketing positioning statements with footnote details make convincing product value statements.

I have made up the following product value statements for GLIDE Floss and ELIXIR Strings as examples.

---

[1] Gore refers to product concept statements. I struggled with the word concept since the concept should advance to an actual product as soon as possible. David Johns coined the phrase, "Product Value Statement," and I have borrowed this phrase with his permission.

Example 1: GLIDE Floss Product Value Statement. Easy to use[1] and clinically proven[2] dental floss that slides easily[3] between teeth without shredding[4].

[1] An application of light beeswax or microcrystalline wax coating to the fiber improves grip. The use of GLIDE Floss is the same as conventional dental floss, and the dispenser lens shows the quantity of floss in the dispenser.

[2] Clinical study completed by the State University of New York Dental School; earned the American Dental Association Seal of Acceptance.

[3] 1150 denier expanded PTFE fiber. The expansion process produces a microporous fibrous structure which gives the product its unique mechanical properties.

[4] A monofilament fiber that does not shred like multifilament fiber.

An engineer might write:

"A dental floss comprising a porous PTFE fiber having a density of less than about 0.7 g/cc. The inventive floss is abrasion-resistant, grippable, and has a soft feel to the hands and a rough feel in the mouth. The floss is made by an extrusion process with non-contact heating during subsequent expansion with amorphous locking."

I copied this text from a Gore dental floss patent claim, proving that patent applications may not be that helpful as a product value statement.

Example 2: ELIXIR Strings Product Value Statement. A coated[1] musical instrument[2] string[3] available at leading music retailers[4] delivering sound quality[5] that lasts[6].

[1] POLYWEB continuous coating serves as a protective barrier against tone-killing dirt and debris that builds up between the windings of a string and reduces wound string corrosion.

[2] Musical instruments include acoustic 6-string and 12-string guitars, electric guitar, electric bass guitar, mandolin, and banjo.

[3] Strings are made by winding round metal wire around a round metal core wire, polishing, grinding (if ground wound), or pressing the exterior part of the winding (if it is a flat wound). Wound wire for acoustic guitar strings is 80/20 bronze metal which is 80% copper and 20% zinc. The wound wire for electric guitar strings is nickel.

[4] Available from local music retailers (~4,000 total), leading chain music retailers, and Internet resellers.

[5] Coated 80/20 acoustic string and electric strings sound like a new conventional guitar string after being played for three hours.

[6] The continuous proprietary coating maintains consistent tone by preventing tone-killing dirt and debris from building up between the windings of a string and reduces wound string corrosion. See US Patent 5801319A.

Nearly every word of an efficient product value statement has a footnote to offer details and explanation. Continue to add details as manufacturing processes take shape, patents are filed and issued, and grassroots sales and marketing campaigns are created.

If regularly updated, the product value statement will help keep the team focused on the customer and the product features that deliver sustainable benefits.

An ongoing challenge is a product that has multiple customer benefits. Pick the most compelling advantage to the customer and focus on this message in your grassroots marketing plan. I had this challenge with ELIXIR Strings. ELIXIR Strings deliver great sound, but they also reduce unwanted fretboard noise, are comfortable, and seem to stay in tune better than conventional guitar strings. We focused on the key benefit, which is string sound and extended musical life.

I revise product value statements as I learn and introduce product improvements. Learning can be the product, the market, market segments, or customer preferences. Bob Gore was a master at doing research quickly, and I remember engaging with a technology team on a personal computer keyboard film protector. The team did a quick-and-dirty water resistance test and assessed whether the film interfered with the keyboard operation. It seemed to work. Bob heard about the idea and bought a package of plastic wrap at the grocery store. It also seemed to work, and we dropped the project with only a few hours invested. Our keyboard protector would never be the "only," which is a lesson in failing fast with quick prototypes. How many presidents of $3B companies would hear about a product idea, go to the grocery store to buy plastic wrap, and let the team know the idea was a bust? Bob Gore was amazing.

The same guidance for product value statements applies if your "product" is a service. A few years ago, my wife, Pamela, and I offered to buy a bar in southwestern Michigan, and fortunately, our offer was low compared to another bid. Our idea was to remodel a failing bar into an intimate restaurant. The menu was simple, and entrées were $15 to $20 with a selective beer, wine, and mixed drink offering. Seating was limited to forty people. A golden rule was no tables next to the restrooms or kitchen. On weekends, a corner of the restaurant would feature a local musician on guitar or keyboards. Many of our ideas came from personal experience in dining at exceptional restaurants in Bucks County, Pennsylvania. There was no comparable restaurant in the region. Our product value statement was "The only intimate restaurant in southwestern Michigan that features cold drinks, warm hospitality, and the best filet and salmon regionally." We called the restaurant "The Cooper Inn," and the signage featured a German Shorthaired Pointer's silhouette. The financial plan was fun to put together, and I learned how hard it is to make money running a restaurant. Lunch, at best, was break-even. We would make money with dinner and drinks. After the deal fell through, Pam and I did not pursue other options to open a small restaurant. We had several issues, including the difficulty in hiring an experienced and reliable general manager and the time available to make this venture a success. Who knows, maybe we dust off this business plan in the future? It sounds like a special place for a nice meal. Building a product value statement for outstanding services is just like a product value statement for a great product.

Product Lifecycle

Everyone knows the product lifecycle.

It is typically a colored chart that plots sales versus time. The first stage is product development, a flat line with no revenue. The second stage is market development, where sales are relatively low but growing slowly. Now the fun begins with the third stage as sales take off rapidly. Rapid sales growth happens in real life for successful products. Now the product lifecycle story takes a sad turn. Stage four is market maturity. Demand is flat, and everyone knows flat sales are bad. But it gets worse. The final stage is sales decline and, worst case, the product's death.

At this point, most people are nodding in agreement, and yes, we have learned this in our Business 101 class. However, I think the product lifecycle's primary use is to protect lousy managers who do not know how to grow their business and have stopped innovating. The classic product example used by these weak managers is the buggy whip that declined in sales as automobile sales grew. Cars were around for more than twenty years before they became commonplace. Twenty years is a lot of time for buggy whip manufacturers to innovate and develop new products with their existing manufacturing capability. I agree with the product lifecycle, but I would insist a successful product line or business is a never-ending series of products that transition from development to decline. I wish

I had a dollar every time managers claim business sales are flat because the products are mature. Shame on you. After all, you stopped innovating.

You need to plan on investing 3% to 5% of sales going to R&D to develop a steady stream of new products. More on this in Lesson 6 – The Important Numbers. Not all products will be successful, so it is best to have multiple irons in the fire.

Intellectual Property

My best advice is to consult with a proven patent and trademark attorney to understand how to protect your intellectual property. This area of law is specialized and can lead to high costs and expensive mistakes if mismanaged.

If you have a unique product, you will likely want to file for a patent in all jurisdictions where you plan on selling the product. I was lucky that Gore employed patent attorneys who not only knew the patent process but were consultants on whether to apply for a patent. I have utility patents and design patents. A utility patent covers the invention of a new product, process, or machine and is enforceable for twenty years from the patent application filing date. Design patents are less costly than a utility patent to file and are enforceable for fifteen years from patent issuance. A design patent protects the exterior of a product.

The GLIDE Floss dispenser is an excellent example of a product with utility patent and design patents. The utility patent covers the invention of a lens that allows for easy viewing of the floss supply and serves as a post for the floss bobbin. In addition, there are two design patents, one with the floss dispenser closed and one with the floss dispenser open showing the lens.

Be aware that you must pay the Patent and Trademark office maintenance fees for utility patents to keep the patent active. Design patents do not have a maintenance fee. Take care when you use an invention publicly the first time. You have twelve months to file for a patent in the United States. Foreign patent rights are far beyond my knowledge, but I understand some countries do not have a twelve-month grace period.

You will likely make some inventions when building a new manufacturing platform for the product. Generally, these inventions are not patented, so that details are not available to competitors. The preferred alternative is to keep the manufacturing invention a trade secret. You should establish process, training, and employee agreements to protect trade secrets from becoming public knowledge. A trade secret that becomes public knowledge means anyone can use your invention.

Trademarks can be confused with copyright. A trademark protects your brand name and logos, and a copyright protects an original artistic or literary work. For example, GLIDE Floss is a registered trademark. We would copyright an advertisement or brochure that explains all the great features. Always be sure that your brand can be a registered trademark.

Now, a counterargument against patents. A patent discloses how to make your product. Creative people will immediately conspire to develop workarounds if your claims have value. How much time and money do you want to spend defending your patent? GLIDE Floss and ELIXIR Strings are patented, but companies worked around claims and launched competitive products within a year or two. Patents for GLIDE Floss and ELIXIR Strings are expired. Today, respected consumer brands and registered trademarks provide ongoing protection. There is a good argument that being first to market and building a powerful brand is more important and valuable than a patent's benefits.

I am suspicious of the claims in some patents. For example, a patent just issued when I committed to developing GLIDE Floss claimed expanded PTFE could only be coated with microcrystalline wax for improved grip. Note the word "only" and a specific mention in the issued patent that no other wax worked. My first action was to buy a sample of every wax available, including beeswax (animal-based), carnauba wax (plant-based), paraffin wax (petroleum-based), and microcrystalline wax (petroleum-based). I set up a simple fiber coating process in a laboratory using a hairdryer to melt the wax and pulled expanded PTFE fiber across the wax for a thin coating. Every wax worked fine. I launched GLIDE Floss using beeswax, not the more popular microcrystalline wax, to avoid conflict with the issued patent. What happened? The patent owner filed a lawsuit against Gore for patent infringement under the theory of doctrine of equivalents. The equivalents doctrine is an interesting legal rule that allows a patent holder to claim infringement even if the alleged infringement is not within the patent claim's scope but is "equivalent" to the patent claim. This rule prevents an infringer from stealing the benefit of a patented invention by making minor changes and retaining the same functionality. The court quickly ruled there was no equivalence doctrine because the patent holder claimed that beeswax did not work, and only microcrystalline wax worked as a coating on expanded PTFE fiber. The patent was garbage and intended to block innovation. In the meantime, Gore had to pay lawyers and spend time in court defending against a patent claim that had no basis.

I end with my beginning suggestion. First, consult with a proven patent and trademark attorney to understand how you will cost-effectively protect your intellectual property.

Competition

I like competition. There is a story of a lawyer who settled in a small town and hung up her shingle. She was the first attorney in the village. After six months, she was ready to pack it up until a second lawyer moved to town, and there was suddenly more business than either could handle. I need to revise the beginning of this paragraph to be "I like competition if I have the best product." Think about two restaurants in town. You can be average but be the preferred establishment if the other restaurant is terrible. I would never suggest anyone try to be "average." Always strive to be "special."

As mentioned above, GLIDE Floss had competition within months of our launch. The products worked but were not as good GLIDE Floss. The alternative floss products were part of an oral health care product portfolio that included higher dollar items like toothbrushes and toothpaste. Dental floss did not get top billing in marketing events or advertising, and the competition did not focus on dental hygienists for marketing.

There was a lack of focus. There were no clinical studies to prove the products worked and no ADA Seal of Acceptance. The fiber denier was too low, allowing lower costs since there were more feet per pound of fiber. Typical feedback from hygienists was, "I tried the competition, but you are so much better. We love GLIDE Floss." From my perspective, the introduction of lower-performing non-shredding floss helped GLIDE Floss succeed.

ELIXIR Strings had a coated guitar string competitor within two years after our launch when our sales were accelerating. The competitor's product was excellent, and their introduction gave credibility to the idea of a coated guitar string. Nevertheless, many musicians remained skeptical whether a coated string can sound great. A credible competitor assured guitar players that the new technology was plausible. Gore no longer had "the only" coated guitar string, but it had "the only" guitar string with a coating covering the entire string, including the gaps between windings. I do not believe having a competitor with a coated string damaged ELIXIR Strings' success; more musicians opted to use coated guitar strings.

It is essential to understand the competition to objectively evaluate your product's benefits and build a compelling product value statement. Nothing good can come from a discussion with your competitors. Stay clear of your competitors at trade events and stay in your lane.

The following is my advice when credible competition arrives, and it will. Evaluate the alternative product, understand your product's differences, and never discuss the competitive product with customers or distribution channel partners. If questioned, acknowledge the product, and begin talking about your product. Time is always the scarcest resource with customers, so use any time to talk about yourself. As I always say, "Enough about me, what do you think about me?" If a competitor violates your patent, engage with legal counsel, and develop a plan of action. The typical first step is a letter from the patent owner notifying the alleged infringer of the patent's existence and the infringing activity. A demand to cease is standard, but you may offer options to resolve the issue in a more friendly manner. I did experience a competitor who was violating an ELIXIR Strings patent claim. Our team elected a prompt, mutually acceptable settlement and moved forward without further distraction.

Lesson 1. Product Lessons

- You do not have a product until you have many satisfied customers and your project is profitable.

- Dream and innovate with your eyes wide open.

- I am most innovative when I do not know what I am doing.

- Create and continually update a crisp product value statement that focuses on the benefits to the customer.

- Product lifecycle is for losers; continually innovate and grow your sales.

- Consult with a proven patent and trademark attorney to understand how you will protect your intellectual property.

- Never brainstorm solutions to a problem or a new product idea with your customer or competitor.

Lesson 2. Your First Business Plan

A Road Map

Your business plan is a road map to document your strategy for the next three to five years and identify critical tactics for the following year. It details your objectives and how you will deal with uncertainty. Unfortunately, every plan is different. The format might be similar, but the content is unique to your product. It will be a valuable tool for your team if you spend the time to make it compelling and insightful. If it is simply good, it will be filed away and might be retrieved when someone asks about the "plan."

Launching a new product is like putting together a puzzle. You have the pieces, but they must be put together for a winning new product launch. Problem-solving is a skill to completing a puzzle, just like launching new products. You will have many assumptions that have to be proven. Be flexible as you learn.

Ninety Days!

It is helpful to create your first business plan in the first ninety days. Writing a business plan will force you to think critically, and you will better understand what you know and what you must learn.

Early in the GLIDE Floss project, I updated my business plan every two months. GLIDE Floss was my first product launch, and I copied Ritchie Snyder, my mentor and coach, on each revision. I spoke with Ritchie every few days, and in one meeting, he questioned why my strategy was constantly in flux. My updates did not clarify that I changed tactics as I learned, but the strategy was the same. I was living and breathing GLIDE Floss, and I made many minor changes nearly every day. Sharing too many updates with relatively minor changes is not valuable. Do not do this! Only share revisions that have significant differences from the previous revision and highlight the updates. Make it clear if your strategy is changing or if only tactics and action plans are revised.

I frequently reflect on the four stages of learning[2] in a new product launch. Stage 2 is the most crucial. Figure 2.1 is a graphic of the four stages.

Figure 2.1. Stages of Learning

3		2
Know What You Know		**Know What You Don't Know**
Do Not Know What You Know		**Do Not Know What You Don't Know**
4		1

Learning to tie your shoelaces demonstrates the four stages of learning. As a young child, what do you care about

_____

[2] "Four Stages for Learning Any New Skill" theory developed at Gordon Training International.

tying shoelaces? You are at Stage 1 in the learning journey to tie your shoes, and this skill is not even on your radar. You do not know that you do not know how to tie your shoes.

You turn five years old, and Stage 2 of learning arrives with surprise and disappointment. Your parents have purchased athletic shoes for you, and they have laces instead of Velcro straps. The problem is you do not know how to tie your shoelaces. One of my early memories is being in a kindergarten class with a three-foot-tall wooden red boot that the students used to learn to tie shoelaces. How many ways are there to tie your shoelaces successfully? According to Ian Fieggen, sixty-two different methods work[3]. Who knew? You are in Stage 2, and you know that you do not know how to tie your shoelaces. Stage 2 is the best stage of learning because your mind is open to new ideas. During a product launch, you must question current practices and build a strategy and tactics to achieve business goals. I love Stage 2 of learning.

Success arrives, you have achieved Stage 3 of learning, and you know how to tie your shoelaces. With Ian's help, you may know sixty-two ways to tie your shoelaces. As a child, you might brag about tying your shoelaces. I offer a warning about Stage 3 of learning. Once you believe you know something, you might stop questioning options. Achieving Stage 3 of learning is troublesome if you stop innovating.

Stage 4 is you do not know what you know. How many adults note their ability to tie shoelaces as a skill? None that I know, and it would be weird if a person bragged about tying

---

[3] See https://www.fieggen.com/shoelace/lacingmethods.htm

shoelaces. That person needs to get out more often. In Stage 4, you do not know that you know how to tie shoelaces. There are thousands of skills we learn and then forget that we know them. How about tying a square knot? I know how to tie a square knot, but it only occurs to me when I need to tie a secure knot. But learning how to tie a square knot was a big deal to me when I was nine years old and just learning how to camp and boat.

As I mentioned, Stage 2 is the best. I am attracted to new products, new markets, new technologies, and building new business support functions because I enjoy questioning the status quo. Stage 2 is a puzzle. It is important to learn the standard process to decide when and how to be different. Talk with experts, but always be skeptical of their opinions. Experts are only as good as their experiences. Worse still, many are so confident in their knowledge that they already know what is possible. I have never been more creative than when I do not know what I am doing.

Stage 2 learning is empowering. There are no rules. You discover pieces of the puzzle and begin to understand the bigger picture. You must be willing to learn fast and quickly recover from small mistakes. A successful product launch requires passion, focus, and urgency. These traits will allow you to learn more quickly.

I bet GLIDE Floss and ELIXIR Strings would not have been launched or successful if experts in these markets and products led the efforts. Both products needed severe disruption to be successful. You had to be naïve to understand preconceived notions of value and technology were wrong.

When did Gore first explore using expanded PTFE fiber in dental floss? 1971. Gore leaders visited consumer product companies for twenty years without success. Expanded PTFE fiber pricing ended discussions. People who knew the market balked at the price of Gore fiber compared to nylon. Nylon was pennies compared to the dollars of expanded PTFE. Experts in the field did not see the value. They had stopped learning and did not value what dental professionals and consumers wanted. Experts and incorrect assumptions of value delayed GLIDE Floss for over twenty years. This delay worked out nicely for me.

Format

I do not worry too much about the format of a business plan. Content and critical thinking are the reasons to create a plan, and the format is secondary. Many companies have a prescribed outline, so use it. There are ten million books available on how to write a business plan. I suggest you buy two books for reference with five-star reviews and be sure the books focus on startups. A business plan for an ongoing business or corporate function is entirely different.

I had no requirement to write a business plan for launching GLIDE Floss or ELIXIR Strings. I built plans for each product launch because it helped me focus. Business plans must be living documents and updated every three months or so during the first two years.

My business plans include:

- Summary

- Products and Services

- Marketing, Brand Management, Sales, Distribution

- Operations

- Technology and Intellectual Property

- Financial Plan

- Critical Issues, Key Risks, and Mitigation

- Timing and Critical Milestones

I grade the quality of a business plan by the summary and the list of critical issues. I limit my summary to one page, and it becomes the outline for the project elevator pitch for internal selling. My best business plans are less than twenty pages. I put all the background or supporting information in an appendix that might be another hundred pages. My mistake in the first ELIXIR Strings plan was to include everything I had learned about string design, market segments, competition, and other interesting but unnecessary details. There is a natural desire to impress people with how much you know. Rather, impress people with what they need to know. I moved 90% of the ELIXIR Strings plan's content to the appendix and substantially improved my focus and document quality.

Collecting Information

The first step in writing a business plan is to collect information. Be sure you understand your product's benefits and weaknesses and know your customer before beginning detailed research. The amount of information available today is staggering, and you will need to focus your search on what is essential.

I begin with the market and identify the competition. You will quickly learn how your product stacks up to alternatives. I like to know the market size early and if any market segments need special attention. Early in your planning, you will estimate annual unit sales and price and calculate the revenue forecast. I have seen new products that forecast a 50% market share in just a few years. Sorry, but this is not going to happen. Market size helps you calibrate your five-year sales forecast. I was somewhat manipulative in my first GLIDE Floss sales forecast. At three years, the market share forecast was about 3%. I generally try to under-promise the revenue forecast and over-deliver, but this can create huge issues for manufacturing planning. I discuss this further in Lesson 6, The Important Numbers.

I enjoy learning about the competition, which is critical to developing your strategy. You must decide which competitor practices you will copy and where you are different. For example, a leader in musical instrument strings is D'Addario. I like this company. D'Addario has an artist relations program that is best-in-class. When building the ELIXIR Strings business plan, I studied every guitar string company's artist relations program. I interviewed music retailers and learned they assumed every leading entertainer or band endorsed D'Addario guitar strings.

Our team did not have the budget or staff to implement a D'Addario style artist relations program. So, during the ELIXIR Strings launch, I focused on building an artist relations program with exceptional and successful musicians who play at festivals, clubs, and churches. The best guitar players are not always household names. Check out music from Larry Pattis (larrypattis.com), El McMeen (elmcmeen.com), Pete Huttlinger (petehuttlinger.com), Kate Wallace (katewallace.com), Michael Camp, Michael Lille (michaellillemusic.com), and Evans & Doherty (evansanddoherty.com). They are talented songwriters, incredible guitar players, and early ELIXIR Strings endorsers.

It is essential to benchmark your competitors. I list competitor information in four categories:

- Company Information. Including headquarters location, leadership, sales, margins, ticker symbol (if public).

- Sales. List SKU sales or regional presence using a pie chart or bar chart. The text includes bullets for context, including strengths and weaknesses. This information can be hard to come by for companies. A good data source is LinkedIn's biographies, and retail product sales data is available for purchase.

- Products. A summary of products, pricing, and other details.

- Other. Miscellaneous details or additional relevant information.

Include competitor information in the business plan appendix. It will be a handy reference in business reviews.

Summarizing the market allows you to decide how you are unique from the competition. You must choose how your product or service will be memorable and stand out in a crowded field. GLIDE Floss and ELIXIR Strings are breakthrough products—a new fiber for floss and a coated guitar string. The products themselves, and pricing, were highly disruptive to customers and channels. You buy the product at the same retailers as the competition. Use instructions for the products were the same as conventional products. Retail packaging was similar but better than the competition. You know you are in trouble if your product's use is different from the incumbent product. A few years ago, an inventor sent me a sample of a new dental floss product. The dental floss package looked like a book of matches from the old days. You would remove a "match" and then pull both ends while it stretched to about eighteen inches in length. Now you are ready to floss. It is unusual, but just being different is not always better.

An essential lesson in collecting information is to talk to people. Get out of the office! Research on the Internet is easy compared to visiting with consumers at events or making appointments with busy retailers. Never assume the market is the same country to country.

SWOT

Before you begin writing your business plan, take a step back and think critically. I use Strength-Weakness-Opportunity-Threat (SWOT), credited to Albert Humphrey and developed in the 1960s. The following diagram shows the SWOT flow.

Figure 2.2. SWOT

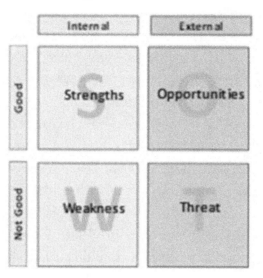

I like SWOT analysis because it forces me to look at internal opportunities and weaknesses versus external opportunities and threats. Some people get hung up on whether the weakness is an opportunity and internal versus external. Do not worry about it. Just brainstorm a list, preferably with a small team of people. Use a proven facilitator if available.

Begin the exercise by looking at "you" (internal)—your strengths and weaknesses. What are your company, your project, or your team strengths? Be careful. Do not start listing the obvious, like you know how to use Excel or make a great pumpkin pie. I do make a great pumpkin pie, by the way. What strengths differentiate your company, your project, or your team and help you achieve success? Build on these strengths in your plan.

Next, what are your company, product, or team weaknesses? Be objective. If your team is not great, say so. If your team is not flexible, creative, or responsive, then list it. Weaknesses are challenging because you must be honest and transparent. I believe the best key strategic issues result from weaknesses and opportunities. Perhaps like mistakes and failures, you can learn a lot from being self-aware and knowing your weaknesses.

Now think outside your company, product, or team. What are the opportunities and threats? I wish I had a dollar every time a team member insists a weakness is an opportunity. Of course, every flaw is an opportunity. I guess some people are more sensitive about the word weakness. For example, let's say you lack specific engineering experience to automate production. Engineering and manufacturing process capability is a weakness. Discussing this issue may lead to an awareness that you lack a process for interviews and onboarding, another weakness for SWOT discussion.

Opportunities have external factors that you cannot control, and the best source of prospects is your competition's weaknesses. GLIDE Floss was a standalone product for Gore, and dental hygienists received clear ongoing communication. High technology dental floss was an add-on product for our competitors. The GLIDE Floss connection with dental hygienists was intimate compared to our competition.

External threats are easy to differentiate from internal weaknesses. For example, you might be concerned with new government tariffs or trade agreement uncertainty. Government regulation can be inconsistent and pose a threat.

You cannot control the threat, but you can prepare to minimize the negative impact of unpredictable government regulatory activity. I expect many SWOT analyses going forward to list a future pandemic as an external threat.

SWOT is also an excellent team-building exercise. An active SWOT discussion is much better than engaging in personality tests, taping a person to a wall, or building a bridge over a creek with toothpicks. SWOT will align the team on capabilities and critical challenges. You may not be able to predict external opportunities or threats early in a new project. Do not sweat it. Early in a project, make SWOT a six-month team exercise, update your observations, and assess your strategy. The first SWOT exercise might take four hours or more if you have a healthy discussion. Update the SWOT every six months in just a couple of hours. The purpose is to inspire the team to think.

Critical Issues

SWOT is an excellent tool to help you prioritize critical issues and assumptions. For example, SWOT might identify a dozen or more pressing matters. A dozen concerns are too many, so rank the issues by those keeping you up at night, and the top four or five will make the most significant difference between success and failure. Then, you will prioritize the work to focus on the most critical actions.

I like to include a sentence or two on mitigation or an action plan to deal with the critical issue. For example, a critical early risk in the GLIDE Floss launch was whether dental hygienists would refer the product to their patients, and if the patients would go to the store to purchase the product. The action plan was to cooperate with a retailer to conduct a regional sales test. I also included customer service as an early critical issue because I was a one-person team. Early in the project, the Gore Fabrics Division customer service helped me with limited customer calls. Later, I set up a customer service team using temporary employees. Finally, our team hired a customer service team with full-time employees after we launched GLIDE Floss nationally.

An early critical issue in ELIXIR Strings was manufacturing automation to ensure consistent quality and lower manufacturing costs. Therefore, the mitigation plan included hiring an experienced process engineer to lead the automation full-time before the launch.

You will be learning about your product, the market, competition, grassroots marketing and sales, manufacturing, technology, intellectual property, and hundreds of other activities as you prepare to launch. Revisit your critical issues every few months to continue to be focused. If your critical issues do not change, you need to be more specific in your mitigation plan to resolve concerns before launch.

Start Writing the Plan

I begin writing once I understand the product, the market, and complete a SWOT analysis. I start by writing the Summary. Mark Twain said it best—"If you want me to give you a two-hour presentation, I am ready today. If you want only a five-minute speech, it will take me two weeks to prepare." My Summary is one page, 10-point font with standard margins—every word matters. You will make choices for product descriptions, marketing initiatives, and critical issues. Focus!

You must be able to explain your business plan in under two minutes. The Summary must be limited to critical matters. For example, manufacturing and operations may not be an issue. Do not include it in the Summary. Gore was already an expert in manufacturing the fiber in the GLIDE Floss business. I outsourced Gore's fiber conversion into dental floss to an experienced retail manufacturing and packaging company. I do not mention Gore's expertise in fiber manufacturing in the Summary. Yes, it is in the plan, but it is not critical to the story or risks. On the other hand, efficient manufacturing operations and automation were critical to ELIXIR Strings' financial success and an essential Summary element.

As previously noted, the following is my outline for writing a business plan.

- Summary
- Products and Services
- Marketing, Brand Management, Sales, Distribution
- Operations
- Technology and Intellectual Property
- Financial Plan
- Critical Issues, Key Risks, and Mitigation

- Timing and Critical Milestones

Spend a lot of time developing your product value statement, discussed in Lesson 1: The Product. It takes time to draft a compelling value proposition. It is a road map for communications by marketing and sales teams if you do it right. I have a friend who hopes to open a fitness gym someday. Just now, it is an idea without a plan. At different times, I ask why his gym would be unique. He knows what he wants to do but cannot yet express why a customer would care. He is smart and will figure it out, and it will become his value proposition.

Questions to Spark Ideas and Issues

Launching a new product can be overwhelming. Take care to prioritize activities and focus on the right actions at the right time. In the GLIDE Floss story, my colleagues in Germany chose to focus on building a high-capacity consumer distribution capability. The capability was impressive. The only problem was they had not spent time understanding how to get orders.

You must prioritize and make choices nearly every day in the launch. Not all products have the same priorities because critical issues are different for each product. Wouldn't it be great if every new product launch had the same challenges? Not a chance. For example, launching a new product in a new market will require more broad activities. GLIDE Floss and ELIXIR Strings fit this model. Once GLIDE Floss was the top-selling dental floss, we continued to develop a range of new floss products like GLIDE Tape, GLIDE Threader Floss, and single-use sachets. Like all new products, the journey begins with product integrity and performance. GLIDE Tape and single-use sachets failed. Consumers did not want GLIDE Tape, and we discontinued the sale of single-use sachets due to manufacturing quality challenges. But these new dental floss SKUs were less challenging to launch because we had a foundation in marketing, sales, intellectual property, finance, and manufacturing for GLIDE Floss.

ELIXIR Strings has a similar story. Our first category was ELIXIR Strings with POLYWEB Coating, and we followed this product line with ELIXIR Strings with NANOWEB coating. POLYWEB strings have a warm tone and are more balanced in the mid-range than the brighter tone of NANOWEB strings. Musician sound preference decides the string selection. I prefer NANOWEB strings, but I am not a good guitar player, so who cares?

Project management systems are a blessing and a curse. Never let your project management system questions wag the tail. It is a tool that can help you identify gaps and set priorities. Many companies have adopted a formal stage-gate decision tool for new projects with standard questions discussed at a gate review. I like any process that helps me make better decisions and to go faster. However, I did participate in a new product review process that was a joke. It included fifty pages of questions to be answered. Okay, maybe not fifty, but too many pages of questions. Rules are rules, and the product leaders "completed the form" with wild guesses rather than saying, "I do not know and need to learn."

Be careful how you use the following summary of questions I like to address before the product launch. Do not let the tail wag the dog.

Products and Services

- List the products and services with specifications.

- What is the product value proposition?

- What is the positioning statement for the product?

- What is the plan for intellectual property (patents, trade secrets, confidentiality agreements, etc.)?

- How soon can the product be sold?

- Has product comparison test data been collected?

- Has a UPC, Universal Product Code, been assigned to each SKU?

- Are there opportunities to expand product offerings?

Market

- Who is the customer?

- Who is the launch customer?

- Who is the competition?

- What competitive response do you expect?

- What is the brand strategy?

- What are the market segments?

- What are the barriers to entry?

- What is the product warranty?

<u>Manufacturing / Operations</u>

- Do we have the capability and capacity to make the product?

- Is there a manufacturing ramp-up?

- Is the process developed and qualified?

- Are manufacturing quality systems required (e.g., ISO Standards, Current Good Manufacturing Process (CGMP))?

- Has direct labor, training, and special skills requirements been determined?

- What is the bill of materials (BOM) for each product SKU?

- Are there raw material supply issues?

- Are there any special shipping requirements?

- Are there any ergonomic issues or concerns?

- Are there any permitting or environmental issues?

- Is product packaging finalized?

<u>Marketing / Sales / Distribution</u>

- Have market segments been identified?

- How will we promote the product?

- Is pull-through marketing an option with a clear reference set that will recommend the product?

- What are the alternative ways to promote?

- Is there a rolling twelve-month integrated marketing and sales plan?

- Is the selling strategy push or pull?

- Is there a reference set to pull-through sales?

- Are sales tools required?

- What is the training plan for salespeople?

- What are the distribution channel options?

- What distribution channel(s) will we use for the introduction?

- What are the markups throughout the channel?

- What are your credit terms, and how is this managed?

- What is your guess of the product's value price compared to the competition?

- What is the anticipated competitive response?

- What is the pricing structure (e.g., Free On Board (FOB) destination indicates price includes delivery at the Seller's expense to a specified location, quantity discounts)?

- Is the pricing plan legal?

<u>The Team</u>

- Is the product launch team staffed, including sales and marketing, customer service, manufacturing, and engineers?

- What is the five-year hiring plan?

<u>Financial</u>

- What are the estimated variable costs at different volume levels?

- What are the estimated fixed costs from Year 1 to Year 5?

- What are the service and return costs?

- What is the likely five-year sales forecast?

- Will capital investment be needed to meet the revenue forecast?

- What are the financial guardrails based on forecasts and estimated costs?

- Is WIP and finished goods inventory effectively managed?

My Favorite Business Plans

I have written dozens of business plans. I wrote my first business plan for a polymer manufacturing startup as an engineer and plant manager at W.L. Gore & Associates in Newark, Delaware. I recall that the business plan was just okay. I am pleased that I recognized the need for a business plan, but it should have included polymer manufacturing and technology center-of-excellence. Ongoing businesses, corporate functions, and new product launches benefit from a written plan.

The GLIDE Floss project was my first attempt to write a serious business plan. My mentor requested I schedule a business review after just three months. Twelve weeks can go by fast if you are drinking from a fire hose. My objective in the plan was to promise just enough that leadership would approve the funding to move forward with an incredibly disruptive business model. Today, I would judge this as an "okay" business plan. I projected five-year sales to be $3M with two employees. My sales forecast and staffing were unrealistic, and I think everyone knew it was just a wild guess. The crucial discussion topic was Gore selling a finished dental floss product to retailers since the company had no experience selling a consumer product. I had many more questions than answers, which is typical early in a new endeavor. Who would have guessed that GLIDE Floss 50-meter mint-flavored package would be the number-one-selling dental floss SKU in the United States in just sixteen months after launch?

My GLIDE Floss business plan was relatively short and crisp.

- The ONLY dental floss that slides easily between tight contacts without shredding.

- A Gore-branded finished product, GLIDE Floss, sold in drugstores.

- Focus on grassroots marketing and sales with reliance on strategic sampling to dental hygienists for pull-through marketing.

- Break-even sales in three years. I guessed the retail value was $2.25 a package, almost $1.00 more than the most expensive dental floss. We launched with an MSRP of $3.50 a package, and you can see I learned quite a bit about product value before the launch.

I updated the GLIDE Floss plan every two to three months with new tactics. But, except for expanding sales to mass merchants and grocery stores, the strategy did not change.

The first revision of the ELIXIR Strings business plan was embarrassing and, thankfully, was not circulated. I attempted to document everything I knew. It was not a helpful plan because it had too much detail about the guitar strings market, competitors, and product development action plan. Fortunately, I cleaned it up before our first critical review. In a nutshell, the business plan discussed:

- The ONLY guitar string offering "sound quality that lasts."

- A Gore-branded finished product sold in chain music stores, independent music stores, and catalogs.

- Focus on grassroots marketing and sales, including alliances with guitar manufacturers to feature ELIXIR Strings with a hangtag. Note: this was unrealistic, and I updated the launch plan to sample guitar instructors and our beta testers for pull-through marketing and trade print advertisement for brand recognition.

- Focus on operational efficiency and manufacturing automation.

- Break-even sales in three years. I guessed the retail value was $15 a set, which was five times the price of conventional guitar strings.

We launched ELIXIR Strings with a suggested price of $15 a set. Value pricing is art and science, and I discuss the pricing process in Lesson 3: Price, Price, Price. Break-even sales took two years, and it was a difficult two years. It takes time for players to accept new technology, and early sales were slow. Internet trolls did not help matters much with misinformation.

The best business plan I have written so far was for an exceptionally disruptive business to sell outerwear featuring GORE-TEX and WINDSTOPPER fabrics. The strategy had too many words, but it was creative and focused on creating sustainable value. The new business model filled a gap in outerwear design, cost, and channel. Our revenue projections were optimistic but not unrealistic. Here is the plan:

- Lifestyle outerwear featuring GORE-TEX and WINDSTOPPER fabrics at leading retailers, including department stores;

- Gore-branded outerwear, and in Year 3, retailer private-branded option;

- Rely on GORE-TEX brand awareness and creative outerwear design, with competitive pricing;

- Develop creative grassroots alliances with non-profit organizations and other companies;

- Break-even sales in two years;

- Reinvent the outerwear value chain to reduce the time from design to sales from eighteen months to six months.

Ironically, my best business plan was a personal failure. Leadership stopped the project before a single sale because it was just too disruptive. A good business plan does not guarantee success, but a flawed strategy and poor execution will guarantee failure. So, to set the record straight, I failed to sell this project effectively to sustain leadership support.

A few years ago, I built and led a new Government Contract Compliance function in the Eaton Law Department. As mentioned, I am most comfortable when I do not know what I am doing. It is empowering to be ignorant since there are no rules, you can ask any question, and you must be open to new ideas to succeed. It is not an exaggeration that I knew nothing about US government contracts when my manager offered me the position. I was interested in the opportunity but told my manager I was not qualified. My manager responded with, "You will learn"—an excellent compliment. You must be a student and open your mind to new and disruptive ideas when building anything new. Be creative. Innovate. Sure, copy the best practices that make sense. That is the easy part. The challenging part is deciding how you will be different and effectively communicate this to your customer.

In a nutshell, I learned that all compliance programs (1) build a written process, (2) teach the process, and (3) confirm that people are using the written instructions. My compliance plan was unique because the key issues were business-focused. My format for an operational or corporate function business plan focuses on three to five key challenges. For Government Contracts Compliance, I selected (1) grow sales and protect margins, (2) create a learning environment, and (3) implement effective controls as my vital strategic issues. It was a helpful business plan.

One learning I had in writing the Government Contract Compliance business plan is setting appropriate expectations. I began the project with words like "best-in-class" and "gold standard." I quickly learned that we would need to hire hundreds of people to pull this off. Government acquisition regulations and accounting requirements are too complicated. I advised company leadership to accept minor findings in government audits that are easily corrected. Effective process, training, and controls will avoid significant findings that have expensive correction plans and penalties.

Project Reviews

When I joined Gore, leadership conducted project reviews to approve a proposed investment. The meeting was called a "critical review." The name was changed to "opportunity review," probably in response to someone sensitive to the word "critical." This name change was the beginning of the end of challenging project discussions. If you want a better plan, assemble intelligent people and conduct a critical review. If the reviewers are thoughtful, the debate will quickly focus on the strategy or tactics' weak links, and they will help you understand the right questions to ask to resolve uncertainty.

The first review of GLIDE Floss was the most challenging product launch business review in my life. No question since it was my first business review. I had worked on GLIDE Floss for just a few months, and I still had more questions than answers. I visited every company that sold dental care products to retailers, and there was no hope of selling expanded PTFE fiber as a branded component. These companies' experts were confident that dental floss could not sell for more than a 15% price premium. My breakthrough moment in GLIDE Floss was the belief that the product was worth more than $2.00 a package and that Gore could sell a consumer product in the retail channel. GLIDE Floss could make money, and the project was worth pursuing.

I assembled Gore's best leaders for the first GLIDE Floss review, including Bob Gore, the Chairman and Chief Executive Officer of Gore, and Ritchie Snyder. Attendees had built the company's three new divisions following Bob Gore's invention of expanded PTFE. Shanti Mehta led Gore's corporate finance function and participated in the review. Shanti had developed a summary of Forms, Numbers 0 to 5, for five-year financial planning to develop my first income statement. He called the forms a Business Development Report (BDR). I created a spreadsheet from Shanti's guidance, and I was off to the races with Shanti as my coach. I had little finance experience, and Shanti and his forms allowed me to understand new product finance basics.

The GLIDE Floss review was contentious, but leadership gave me the green light to further develop a Gore-branded consumer product in a new market and then advised me that the competition would crush me. I was excited, and I had permission to develop a Gore-branded consumer product. I was confident that I had a winning business strategy.

Gore leadership helped me better understand the weak links in my business plan, and I continued these reviews with senior executives every six months for the next two years. There was no requirement for these follow-up meetings. I scheduled the meetings because they helped me build a better plan.

The ELIXIR Strings critical reviews were the same but different. My first business review for ELIXIR Strings was at seven in the morning, next to the Little America Hotel's swimming pool in Flagstaff, Arizona. I had just finished breakfast in the hotel restaurant and walked to Lodge 4 to pick up my laptop and drive to the plant. I ran into Bob Gore, said hello, and Bob asked how I was doing. As mentioned, Bob is the Chairman and Chief Executive Officer of Gore. I explained that a small team was working part-time on ELIXIR Strings and making good progress. Bob had seen an early prototype of the guitar string, and I understood he was not particularly impressed. We spoke for about fifteen minutes, and Bob was anxious to learn more about the project.

Bob's first question was the product value statement (e.g., the value proposition). The product value was sound quality that lasts. He wanted to know how we measured sound quality, coating wear, the market size, competition, and value pricing assumptions. *We are still learning.* Bob asked whether we had a physics expert on the team to research vibrations and waves? *No, we did not.* Do you have a brand? *Not yet.* Has a patent been filed? *It is in process.* Is the manufacturing process stable and efficient? *Not yet.* I remember assembling our small team that day and relaying Bob's questions. Bob helped our team focus, and he asked excellent questions. We recruited a Gore Associate to work part-time on the team who was an expert in physics and concentrated on the science of guitar string vibrations and waves. My memory is this conversation resulting in Dave Myers inventing the "pick-o-matic" to measure coating wear. Dave invented ELIXIR Guitar Strings. Dave built a simple tool that would pick a guitar string a selected number of picks, and a technician would measure the coating's wear to a calibrated scale.

The first scheduled ELIXIR Strings critical review was about two months later, and Bob Gore attended. All team members participated in the meeting, and it was a team-building event. I had lost my voice that day and could barely speak. Maybe this was good? By the end of the meeting, my responses were visual. A nod here and there, a few spoken words, and a thank you. It was a critical review, and our plan was better for it.

I despise the devil's advocate in a business review. A devil's advocate offers an absurd opinion to provoke a response and, in theory, a vibrant discussion. My experience is that only dullards resort to offering stupid views to start a debate. There are too many good questions that can drive the conversation. Do your best to exclude managers who like to be a devil's advocate, and I am so pleased I could use the word "dullard" in this lesson.

Also, beware of the *kumbaya* business review. A kumbaya review is over-the-top friendly, and leadership is acting as a cheerleader to motivate the team. I hate this. A helpful review should be challenging and make you think. I have no time for a meeting to sit around a campfire and sing folk songs. Not helpful.

Dashboards

Once you have a plan, build a simple dashboard that lists each initiative, expected timing, and use a green-yellow-red bowling chart to show your progress. A bowling chart is a simple summary of initiatives followed by a color indicating progress. Green means the activity is on track. Yellow means there are issues or challenges. Red means there are severe problems with the initiative. Team meetings must focus on yellow and red items, with no discussion of green activities. Time is too valuable to remind people there are no issues.

Update the dashboard monthly. It will take less than thirty minutes if you are focused. Include who is taking the lead on initiatives, timing, and include a column for remarks. Simple is always better.

Dashboards are your friend. If done right, they do not take too much time to update, and you can tell how you are progressing.

Lesson 2. Your First Business Plan Lessons

- The purpose of a business plan is to help you and your team be successful; a secondary benefit is more effective communication with leadership and stakeholders.

- Without a business plan, your product is just an idea, and the idea is going nowhere.

- Take time to research before writing your business plan.

- SWOT is an excellent team-building event and will help you identify critical issues, key assumptions, sustainable competitive advantage, and other opportunities and risks.

- Your business plan must be a clear road map of how, when, and where you will launch and commercialize your product; a good plan resolves uncertainty.

- Be passionate and focused, with a scary sense of urgency when writing your plan.

- Harsh reviews with intelligent people will make a better business plan.

- Use a simple dashboard with a bowling chart to communicate business plan initiatives' progress.

- Your business plan's one-page summary is the best internal communication tool for your new product launch.

Lesson 3. Price, Price, Price

My Coach and Mentor

I am reminded of Ritchie Snyder, my coach and mentor, whenever product pricing is a topic. Ritchie was a pricing guru, and when he mentioned pricing, he would always repeat it three times, "price, price, price." Sometimes he would whisper "price, price, price" for effect. Ritchie recognized the benefits Gore products offered to our customers, and he was fearless in asking for a fair price. He lived and breathed value pricing, not "high" prices.

I have a Ritchie story that might be folklore, but I like the story. Early in his career at Gore, leadership requested Ritchie assess the path forward for a struggling business and possibly exit the market. The business had declining sales and margins for years, and the value proposition was perceived to be weak. Ritchie joined the business and interviewed the team, who confirmed the worst. The business was at its end-of-life. Remember the product lifecycle? Ritchie traveled to customer locations, discussed the benefits of the product, and posed the possibility of Gore exiting the business. Customers freaked out when learning of the option of discontinued sales. The business had overreacted to distributor price complaints and lowered the price for several years to respond to these criticisms. As a result, leadership lost faith in the value of their product.

Ritchie got the team together and proposed a disruptive plan to win in the future. He doubled the price of every product. Life is unpredictable. Orders did not slow, and they grew with time. The team launched additional products with the new value pricing, and revenue growth continued to increase. Once again, the business was a success story with outstanding margins, and Ritchie became a value pricing legend. Most general managers would have accepted a mistaken assessment of product value, may have looked for options to lower costs to increase margins, and then exited the business and declared victory.

Pricing for a new product, especially disruptive products, looks easy if done correctly. Product pricing has become a professional specialty in large companies, and I do not pretend to know penetration, economy, skimming, or the dozen other pricing strategies developed by intelligent people.

I know two pricing strategies, cost-plus pricing and value pricing.

Cost-Plus Pricing

I never use cost-plus pricing, except when I do. Cost-plus pricing is simple, and anyone can do it so long as you know your costs and have a calculator. For example:

(1) Your new widget's total variable and fixed costs total $1.00.

(2) The company strives for a 20% pre-tax profit.

(3) A new widget price is $1.00 plus 20% of $1.00, which is $1.20.

Cost-plus pricing results in a 20% pre-tax profit. But can you be sure that total variable and fixed costs equal $1.00 for a new product? Not bloody likely. Knowing your costs when you launch a product is challenging. Manufacturing has not been scaled and is inefficient. Overheads are high as a percentage of sales and do not reflect the possible automation investments you will be making in the next two to three years as sales grow.

The more likely methodology for cost-plus pricing with a new product is to match the leading competitor's price.

(1) The existing widget sells for $1.20.

(2) You estimate your widget's variable costs and fixed costs in Year 3 are $1.00.

(3) You match your competitor's price, and the spreadsheet says your pre-tax profit is 20%.

In this example, it is very convenient that 20% profit matches your company's pre-tax profit expectations, and you are finished. But no one is this lucky. A more likely scenario is your widget's estimated variable costs and fixed costs are higher than $1.00.

Let's say the total costs are $1.08. Now you have three choices. Your first option is to believe your variable and fixed costs and charge $1.30 for your widget resulting in a 20% pre-tax profit. Your second option is to match your competitor's price of $1.20 and live with an 11% pre-tax profit. This profit margin is not worth the trouble of a new launch. You are guessing costs, which are likely higher than expected, meaning your pre-tax profit will be less than 11%. The third option is to take immediate steps to lower variable and fixed costs to $1.00 and voilà—you have a 20% margin and matched the price of the leading competitor. Congratulations, the pricing is finished. Cost-plus pricing is more complex than it looks for a new product.

You are an idiot if you base your new product price solely on costs. But, cost-plus pricing can be an excellent strategy with promotional products like dental professional GLIDE Floss samples.

Value Pricing

While I was a Gore Associate, the company practiced value pricing. Value pricing is complicated for a new product and might be more art than science. Gore invented lifesaving vascular grafts and stents. Determining the value price is challenging because what is the value of your life? Fortunately, I only had to assess the value of dental floss, guitar strings, and a failed project—lifestyle outerwear.

Value pricing does not mean "high price," a common misconception.

Value pricing is the fair price a customer is willing to pay. Nobody likes paying too much. In my version of value pricing, the customer and the company share the premium value of the product. The value price will never be the highest price the customer is willing to pay. The customer will decide that the price is fair.

I begin value pricing assessment by listing competitive product offerings as a starting point. I learned a few lessons in conducting focus groups, and the most important learning is that the result is almost always determined by how you ask questions. More than once, I witnessed marketing experts ask whether a product is worth more than their current product of choice? If the answer is yes, the expert then asks how much more? Asking how much more is one of the few dumb questions that exist in the world today. The answer will most likely be, "I would pay 10%, maybe 15%, more for this product." This price premium over a legacy product may not offer the margins you require, and now you are in a bind. Focus group opinions of product value and market experts delayed GLIDE Floss availability for more than twenty years because they believed it was only worth a 15% premium. I launched with a 250% premium. I offer details later in this lesson.

Years ago, I participated in a value pricing seminar. The first exercise was to list a new product's benefits in one column and record the benefit's dollar value in the adjacent column. Now add up the dollars in the benefit column, and you have the price premium. Unfortunately, it does not work this way because most benefits are subjective or qualitative. The exercise suggests advantages are objective and, with a calculator, you have a number. For example, ELIXIR Strings' key advantage is that the coating offers a consistent tone over the string's extended life compared to conventional guitar strings that quickly lose their brightness. The consistent tone and brightness are subjective.

Always remember there are two alternatives for your customer. First, the customer can use the traditional product, and this product becomes the pricing reference point. The second scenario is there is no conventional product, and the reference for value is a decision to continue to do without the product. Today, the second scenario is rare because there are so many alternative products in the market. Thank you, capitalism.

Ask your customer open-ended questions about product value and then listen. You will be surprised at how much you learn.

The final step in value pricing is to compare your costs with the assumed value price and calculate your pre-tax margin to ensure it meets expectations. I prefer a minimum of 30% pre-tax margin early in the project, hoping that reality is never below 20% pre-tax margin. If your projected pre-tax margin is too low, raise your price or lower your costs. It is better to go belly-up if you fail because customers do not accept your price than working hard and not making money.

In summary, your value price shares the value with the customer, and it is a number between the product value and total fixed and variable costs, as shown in Figure 3.1. The customer will be happy and feel they are getting a good deal. I like new products that substitute directly for alternative products. However, some new products may have additional costs for installation, maintenance, or service life. You will need to deduct this cost in your value pricing analysis.

The following diagram is a simple illustration of product value, price, and costs.

Figure 3.1 Product Value, Value Price, and Costs

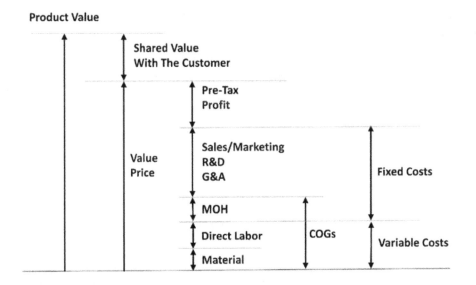

Finally, remember that pricing is not a number. What?

Terms of sale can significantly sway the price. For example, let's say you are selling bricks, and the price is FOB Destination. FOB Destination means you are paying the shipping costs to the customer's delivery location. You'd better be sure your value price analysis includes the cost of shipping heavy bricks. In addition, many companies are attempting to improve cash flow by extending payment terms. In the old days, companies paid for products and materials within thirty days unless offered a discount to pay sooner. It is not unusual for large customers to extend their payment terms to 120 days or more. Good for you; you are now a bank and providing a loan to your customer. Make sure to include the cost of financing your customer in your cost analysis.

The GLIDE Floss story includes a discussion of market segmentation. Market segmentation assumes that not all customers are the same. Market segmentation is targeting a grouping of customers with different product offerings. In GLIDE Floss, there are two segments: consumers and dental professionals. Pricing is different for each market segment, as noted in the GLIDE Floss story below.

GLIDE Floss Value Pricing

Consumer Products

GLIDE Floss was my first opportunity to determine the value price of a new product. In hindsight, I did a good job.

I will begin with the more challenging market segment, consumers who buy dental floss in a retail store. First, consumers have many choices to purchase conventional nylon dental floss, branded and private label, especially in drugstores. The GLIDE Floss launch first focused on large drugstore retailer chains, then expanded sales to mass merchants (e.g., Walmart, Target, Kmart), and finally focused on distribution in grocery stores. Drugstores have higher margin expectations than mass merchants or grocery stores, and I wanted consumers to see the "higher" price at launch. Be careful. As a supplier, you cannot direct the retailer to charge a specific price for a product. The retailer decides the price their customer will pay, but you can influence the retailer with a Manufacturer's Suggested Retail Price (e.g., "MSRP").

The following are critical pricing assumptions for sales of dental floss to drugstore chains:

- Drugstores typically have 50% margins. A 50% margin means you can multiply your price to the retailer by two to estimate the consumer price.

- The consumer paid $1.40 for a 50-yard package of the top-selling dental floss product. Competitors offered lower-price dental floss options, and private-label dental floss was about $1.40 per 100-yard dispenser (e.g., one-half the price per yard of the branded product).

- The dental floss leader sold one unit per week of the top-selling SKU of dental floss, and this metric has always felt low to me. So, a 3,000-store retailer will sell 3,000 units of the top-selling dental floss per week. The price of a product will impact sales if it is too high. Remember, the customer always decides whether the value price is fair.

I talked with thousands of dental hygienists about the consumer price of dental floss while developing the product, and they were my focus group. My first learning was that dental hygienists generally had no idea of dental floss cost in a drugstore. A few did, but they were the exception. Almost all hygienists agreed that GLIDE Floss was worth a premium over nylon dental floss, especially for patients with tight contacts. Tight contacts sound like a niche, but most people have difficulty flossing. How much is comfort worth? Many people experience floss shredding between teeth, sometimes going to the dentist to remove the floss from a tight contact. How much is no snapping of floss into gums while flossing worth? It is impossible to quantify comfort objectively. What is the value of a lens in the floss dispenser that displays the quantity of floss remaining? Since I thought of this improvement, I would say "a lot."

My best discussions with hygienists were not about dollars per package but other reference points. For example, is GLIDE Floss worth five cents a day? Everyone agreed this was a fair price. There was some pushback when regular floss was just one and one-half pennies a day, but then I would bring up the cost of dental tape at three to four cents a day. Suddenly five cents per day seemed more reasonable.

Some conversations were crazy. I remember one group of hygienists was adamant that a package of GLIDE Floss was worth more than a fast-food restaurant value meal. A value meal costs about five bucks at the time. After months of discussions, I believed GLIDE Floss's value was about $3.00 for a 50-yard dispenser. I would share the benefits with my customer, and my initial guess for GLIDE Floss MSRP was $2.25 in a drugstore, just under one dollar more than the top-selling dental floss.

The GLIDE Floss story details a sales beta test in twenty-five Happy Harry's drugstores before our launch. My goal in the test sales program was to challenge my $2.25 pricing assumption and to confirm dental hygienists would refer patients to stores to buy the product. Unfortunately, the retail trial could not wait for the new dispenser, so I used a two-piece round dispenser readily available. I will not repeat the entire story, but we began a twelve-week sales test in January 1992, two SKUs, regular and mint flavor, 50-yards for $2.99. The target was to match the sales of the top-selling dental floss with sales of 600 units.

At the end of the twelve weeks, we sold over 12,000 units. About 60% of sales were mint flavor and 40% unflavored, consistent with traditional dental floss. We could have sold more during the test, but it was challenging to keep the stores stocked. I spent most of my time delivering floss to the Happy Harry's warehouse from our contract manufacturer to restock stores. I was having a ball during this sales test. I changed my opinion of GLIDE Floss's value to be $5.00 per package, and I would launch at $3.50 for 50-meters to share the value with the customer. As previously mentioned, Ritchie suggested we offer 50-meters (54.7-yards) to embrace the metric system. But for this sales test, I would have underpriced GLIDE Floss. A fair price is $3.50 per package, and sales history following the commercial launch nine months later confirmed this. Value pricing is satisfying when you have a happy customer. I continued to stock the beta product in Happy Harry's drugstores until our official launch six months later, and sales far exceeded expectations.

Dental Professional Products

I developed a comprehensive line of products for dental professionals. Offerings included two categories of products: (1) floss for use in the dental practice, including 200-meter vials and 200-meter font refills, and (2) 5-meter, 10-meter, and 15-meter GLIDE Floss samples for dental professionals to give patients following a cleaning.

I considered sales to dental professionals a marketing program, not a sales program. I priced the products used in the dental practice at the same price as a conventional nylon product, a cost-pricing tactic. My logic is that they could replace the nylon floss used in their dental office without considering the price. These products delivered a small margin. I priced the GLIDE Floss samples for dental professionals to give away at cost. I did not make any profit from these sales. In my mind, I was brilliant because the dental office was paying for our consumer sampling program.

Our plant controller would continuously note the low-margin sales to dental professionals in business review meetings. I patiently explained this was a marketing initiative, not a sales program. How many marketing programs pay for themselves? It was like the "Groundhog Day" movie as I explained the rationale for dental professional pricing time and again. Our sales to dental offices were relatively high, which is why the low margins received attention. The pricing protocol for dental professionals stayed in place while I was on the team.

I consider the value pricing to dentists and hygienists to be a great success and would not change anything.

You Are Freaking Me Out

Year 2 of commercial sales and GLIDE Floss mint-flavored and unflavored SKUs are now top-selling products in the United States. We have distribution in all the leading drugstore chains and mass merchants, and the sales team is making good progress with distribution in grocery store chains. Sales are growing monthly, and it is an exciting time for our team.

Our top customer calls Jane Gardner, their Sales Associate, and it is not a long conversation. The buyer politely explains that he will discontinue ordering the product unless Gore immediately lowers GLIDE Floss's price by 15%. The customer explains they will pass the price decrease to the consumer, and they have a responsibility to give the consumer a better deal. Monthly sales are about $500,000 and growing.

Jane calls a GLIDE Floss leadership meeting and explains the situation. Jane knows the account, and they are not bluffing. My first reaction is we are not going to negotiate our price with each chain retailer. It would be impossible to manage, and the first demand of any retailer is they receive the best price. If we caved to the request, we agree to a 15% price decrease across the board. Agreeing to a price decrease encourages a future demand to lower prices.

Jane recommends we advise the retailer that we are not able to lower our price. She will travel to their headquarters to propose additional cooperative promotional investments by Gore and focused communication to dental hygienists of store product availability. We are not optimistic. The buyer was friendly when Jane called him. He said no to any discussion, and electronic orders stopped immediately. Losing our best customer when everything is going well does not make sense.

What do you do?

Jane made weekly calls to the buyer that were not accepted, and the buyer does not acknowledge email communications. Four executives from the retailer stopped by our booth at a trade event. The meeting was brief, and they repeated their pricing request. Jane kept Gore's leadership advised of the situation and our actions. After two months of no orders, we initiated direct mailings to dental hygienists to request retailers offer the product and informed them of the broad list of retailers where their patients could buy GLIDE Floss. Jane continued attempts to reach the buyer without success.

Suddenly, after four months and without notice, we received a large restocking order. Jane called the buyer and received an appointment to discuss new cooperative promotional investments by Gore at their headquarters. Everyone pretended nothing happened, and the retailer once again led monthly sales. You might expect the retailer to have been harsh, but their communication was always professional and respectful. It was scary.

We learned a valuable lesson. Do not lower your value price if your customer makes a request. Lowering your price is a slippery slope. Instead, believe in the value of your product and change your marketing tactics to deal with sales setbacks.

ELIXIR Strings Value Pricing

ELIXIR Guitar Strings is a success story at so many levels. The team was exceptional, and product development was textbook. Innovation was constant, and the product screams "Ordinary People Doing Extraordinary Things." There are many variations on this quote, and Jim Valvano, the basketball coach at North Carolina, is credited with this version. He won the NCAA Men's Basketball Championship game in 1983 as underdogs to the University of Houston Cougars. Also, grassroots marketing worked!

Pricing was even more challenging than GLIDE Floss and a topic of discussion with hundreds of musicians before the commercial launch. The primary sales channel would be independent music stores, not chain retailers. The following are critical pricing assumptions:

- Independent music stores typically have 50% margins. Like the GLIDE Floss assumption, a 50% margin means you can multiply your price to the retailer by two to estimate the consumer price.

- The consumer paid $3 to $4 for leading acoustic guitar strings and $2 to $3 for electric guitar strings. Competition in guitar strings is fierce and is subject to special sales and one-off discounting.

The value proposition of ELIXIR Strings is sound quality that lasts. Great sound is a requirement, and our strings were on par with the leaders in the market. ELIXIR Strings' real value is a consistently excellent tone for three to five times the conventional guitar string's life. What is the value of a guitar that sounds the same regardless of the life of the string? A whole lot to musicians who value tone. Some musicians ask why the string does not last forever since the coating protects the windings from evil contamination? At the time of our launch, a competitor sold used guitar strings that he cleaned with a solvent and repackaged. This idea failed. The answer to guitar string eternal life is they are subject to metallurgical fatigue when tuned. Fatigue will compromise vibration with time, and eventually, the string will break. I remember hearing about a company that invented a single hard drive to store all the Library of Congress materials. How many of these are you going to sell? I have never been a fan of a product that never needs replacement. ELIXIR Strings are mortal but sound consistently great, about five times longer than a conventional string.

ELIXIR Strings reduce unwanted fret noise for many musicians. There is nothing worse than listening to an acoustic guitar squeaking every time the musician changes the chord position with their left hand. How much is this worth? Some musicians prefer this squeak. This benefit does not seem to offer a price premium.

The POLYWEB Coating is easier on the fingers for the casual or new guitar player. What is this worth? Many musicians claim ELIXIR Guitar Strings stay in tune better. I take back my comment on acoustic guitar squeaking above because there is nothing worse than spending time watching a musician tune his guitar during a show between songs. You can see I have remarkably high expectations of professional musicians. As with squeak, these benefits are highly subjective and may not offer a price premium.

Jeannie Guthrie and I visited music events monthly and talked for hundreds of hours with musicians about their preferences and price. Ask any musician about the price, and 99% will want it free. Musicians are a frugal group but will pay for products that perform. Strings are a minimal investment compared to the price they will pay for a guitar.

The bottom line is that I became comfortable with a value of $20 per set. Most musicians only changed their strings monthly, although many professionals claimed to change strings every week. To share the value, our proposed MSRP would be $15 per set. ELIXIR Strings are about four to five times the price of conventional guitar strings at the time.

GLIDE Floss allowed for a controlled sales test in Happy Harry's drugstores. We did not have a reference set like dental hygienists for ELIXIR Strings, and I hoped I correctly guessed the value price. As I mentioned in the ELIXIR Strings story, the first six months following our launch were a frightening time. We have a great product. Musician feedback is excellent. The shock of our pricing seemed to be mostly under control. But sales were lagging. I was having some doubts about whether ELIXIR Strings would be successful. Maybe I screwed up the pricing, and ELIXIR Strings did not have broad appeal at four to five times the price of conventional strings? I credit our integrated sales and marketing plan for sales and reorders and exceeding our business expectations.

For the first eighteen months, music retailers complained loudly about our pricing, which surprised me just a bit. They made $7.50 selling one set of ELIXIR Strings and only made $2.00 for selling one set of conventional guitar strings. They enjoyed an extra $5.50 on each sale. Of course, longer musical life means the next string sale will be weeks later than a conventional guitar string. But musicians may not have changed their strings as much as they claim. It is like flossing. The dental floss market would be twice as big if everyone flossed as much as they claimed.

An established practice in the music market is electric strings cost less than acoustic strings. There are three more costly wound strings in an electric guitar set and four wound strings in an acoustic guitar set. I decided to price our electric guitar strings the same as acoustic guitar strings, $15 per set. There was pushback from music retailers for this decision. I had no problem explaining to owners of music stores and retail chains that ELIXIR Strings was selling sound quality that lasts and that pricing was based on value, not on costs. A few years ago, ELIXIR Strings changed the pricing strategy and discounted electric strings from $15 per set to $12 per set, a 20% price decrease. I think this was a wrong decision, but what do I know? I discuss how many more sets of strings you must sell to make the same amount of money in Lesson 6, The Important Numbers.

ELIXIR Guitar Strings, the first coated musical instrument string that works, was disruptive on many levels. History indicates $15 per set was the right price based on musicians buying the product, compared to the conventional guitar string at $4 per set. The assumed value of $20 per set was a guess. Remember, the customer always decides if your price is fair.

Guitar Manufacturer Sales

Our team was successful in selling guitar strings to guitar manufacturers a few years after launch. Leading guitar manufacturers would install our strings at the factory, and at the time, include a hangtag promoting ELIXIR Guitar Strings.

I can be a victim of repeating past practices that have a happy ending. Can you guess my pricing strategy for guitar manufacturers? I copied my pricing practice for dental floss used in the dental office. ELIXIR Guitar Strings were shipped in bulk to lower packaging costs and sold at the price the manufacturer paid for conventional strings. The price offered a low margin, and the good news is our high margin sales covered the relatively lower volume of sales to guitar manufacturers. Unlike GLIDE Floss, no one made any distracting noise with this pricing strategy. I am pleased with my pricing strategy with guitar manufacturers.

The Barn Coat – Value Pricing With A Twist

I led a new project to sell lifestyle apparel made from GORE-TEX and WINDSTOPPER fabrics that I call "The Barn Coat." The business model in this project was completely different than GLIDE Floss and ELIXIR Strings. Our team was planning to sell lifestyle apparel made from Gore technology fabrics that had been around for more than twenty years. The customer understood the value of GORE-TEX fabrics and the appropriate price premium.

Our pricing for lifestyle apparel recognized Gore technology fabrics' premium value, but costs mostly decided the price. What? Cost pricing in Gore is heresy, and I mentioned earlier that you must be an idiot to use cost pricing. The Barn Coat story is an exception because it was a requirement that Gore laminate customers could sell the same styles with expected margins. Fortunately, several Gore fabrics customers are publicly traded companies, and their annual reports included margin performance for benchmarking.

Pricing of a jacket became a spreadsheet exercise. Gore charged our team the customer price for technical fabrics, and Jeannie Guthrie worked with the team to calculate costs for manufacturing, logistics, and tariffs. We added the profit margin expectation of Gore customers, and that is the price. Our team would show our actual costs to the Gore laminate customer if the products were launched. The assumption is this transparency would reduce objections by laminate customers of Gore selling outerwear. Our team would offer several options to Gore fabrics customers:

(1) Design, manufacturing, and cost details for the laminate customer to manufacture the apparel; or

(2) Our team would make the outerwear for them at a price that would meet their apparel value pricing and profit expectations.

Creating an apparel manufacturing center-of-excellence would have been compelling to retailer-branded apparel since they often did not have the capability or capacity to make additional apparel styles. It would have been interesting to see if this model could be a success.

We did not learn any pricing lessons in The Barn Coat project because we never sold the product. My business model was perceived to be too disruptive to existing customers, and we ended the project. However, sales of biking and running outerwear would continue.

Lesson 3. Pricing Lessons

- Pricing is not a number. Price includes terms of sale, warranty, guarantees, shipping costs, reliability, inventory commitment, total product offerings, qualified salespeople, easy price lists, and early notice of shipping problems.

- Raise your price to the customer annually or when there is an opportunity. If your customer wants anything special, say yes if appropriate and charge for it.

- You are likely an idiot if you base your price solely on costs.

- Value pricing is art and science, and it looks easy if successful. Remember that the customer decides whether your price is fair. Be courageous and confident of your product's value. Share the added value of your product with the customer, and they will always believe your price is fair.

- Talk with hundreds of people to understand the value of your product, but never ask the question, "Do you think it is worth more?"

- Never lower your price in response to a customer request unless you have overestimated the value of your product.

- Explore marketing initiatives that might allow for sales at discounted prices. These customers are paying for your sampling plan.

Lesson 4. Grassroots Marketing and Sales

Integrate Grassroots Marketing and Sales

You can have the best product in the world, and it will likely fail without excellent marketing and sales. Messaging must be crisp. If you do it right, it will look easy, and of course, anyone could do it. Sales, especially in a new market, are more challenging than you think.

My definition of grassroots marketing is practical messaging to a targeted group of customers or influencers. A good marketing program sells the value of your product to your customer. The Sales organization uses consistent and repeated marketing messaging to close the deal and receive an order.

Having credible competition is good. Within a few months of launch, GLIDE Floss competed with two new dental floss products with similar benefits from leading oral health care companies. The alternative offerings gave credibility to our disruptive offering. The good news is their salespeople did not know how to position or sell their improved dental floss. The sales pitch was, "Oh...and we have a new dental floss." Not compelling. Their marketing organization did not talk to sales, and GLIDE Floss was the beneficiary. The companies had a broad dental health product portfolio, and their new dental floss got lost in the mix. Integrating marketing and sales is critical.

In contrast, our team focused on GLIDE Floss, with a grassroots marketing campaign directed to dental hygienists.

Our retail sales team led the grassroots marketing strategy with dental hygienists. You cannot be more integrated than this.

We did sell many different GLIDE Floss SKUs to meet customer needs. Within two years of launch, we sold dental professionals 200-meter refills, 200-meter vials, 15-meter samples with or without the dental practice name, 10-meter patient samples, 5-meter patient samples, GLIDE Floss Tape, and single-use sachets. Retailers could buy 50-meter mint-flavored or unflavored packages, 200-meter vials, a GLIDE Floss holder, GLIDE Floss Tape, GLIDE Threader Floss, with retail promotions in floor displays, counter displays, and end wing displays. Our team offered special promotions like a free 5-meter sample with a 50-meter mint-flavored package, cinnamon-flavored GLIDE Floss, and neon-colored dispensers. All these products and promotions generated positive noise and a reputation for savvy marketing. Our sales team always had something to talk about in calls to retailers.

ELIXIR Strings has a broad product portfolio to meet the needs of musicians. Strings are available for acoustic guitars, 12-string acoustic guitars, electric guitars, electric bass guitars, mandolin, and banjo. Packages came in different gauges. The gauge affects the tension at which a string vibrates to achieve the desired pitch. A light string is more flexible than a medium string and vibrates fast with a bright tone but sustains less than a heavier string. Musicians are fussy and demand their preferred gauge. These SKUs provide marketing and promotional opportunities. Our artist relations program also offered great opportunities to promote our product. Early on, we invested in musician showcases at festivals and music events like the Kerrville Folk Festival and Folk Alliance.

A helpful and straightforward tool for integrating grassroots marketing and sales is a visual twelve-month map of marketing activities and how they relate to sales activities. For example, before a dental trade show, we mailed samples of GLIDE Floss to registered dental hygienists within a zip code region. The mailing included our booth number, plus a reason to visit our booth. Salespeople are aware of the mailing and prepared to discuss a new product or retailer availability. I am a fan of limited magazine advertisements, but the real value is mailing a color reprint of the ad to retailers before a scheduled sales call. Buyers like to get this type of mail and generally assume the ad appears in many magazines. Salespeople are prepared to discuss ad placement and response.

A best practice is no marketing initiatives that do not align with a sales activity. I am also a fan of a single leader for marketing and sales, but this seems rare in larger businesses.

Learn the Market

Before launching a new product, you will spend months learning the market, including market segmentation, distribution channels, alternative offerings, pricing, value, future messaging, distribution, and hundreds of other details. Understanding a market is the fun part of a new product launch. If it is a new market, you have the advantage of not knowing what you are doing. There are no boxes to limit your creativity. You decide when to be different in marketing and messaging and when to be the same as the competition.

A new product must stand out. If everything is the same as the competitive offerings, you will not succeed. You have a product that might only compete on price, which is no fun, in my opinion. I like to be a unique product with a value price.

If everything is different, you will also fail. Messaging for a new product is a balancing act. Too much focus on differences and "a new product category" might make customers less likely to take a risk in using your product. GLIDE Floss and ELIXIR Strings are vastly different from alternatives, but their use is exactly like traditional products. Adoption by dental professionals, consumers, and musicians was no big deal.

You must quickly identify who your customer is. Many people get this wrong or, at a minimum, are confused, and it makes a mess of your marketing. For GLIDE Floss, is the customer the retailer, the dental hygienist, or the consumer with tight contacts? The dental hygienist recommends GLIDE Floss to their patients. But dental professionals are also customers. They use dental floss in their practice, and this requires unique packaging like 200-meter floss refills that fit office-type dispensers. Many dental offices offer their patients samples, and we sold dental professionals 15-meter, 10-meter, and 5-meter dispensers to give to their patients following an exam. Dental practices buy the product directly from the manufacturer or distributors' network. Dental professionals are customers. The retailer is also an important customer and critical to the consumer purchasing the product. Consumers want GLIDE Floss because it slides easily between tight contacts without shredding. You can have multiple customers and differentiate marketing and sales initiatives depending on the customer or segment. I know some marketing experts consider retailers to be a distribution channel partner, not a customer. I disagree. Treating retailers like customers will more likely result in improved focus, respect, and communication.

ELIXIR Strings segments and customers are like those of GLIDE Floss. Musicians are customers who care about sound quality that lasts. Music stores are customers who need reliable supply and a product that delivers acceptable margins. Musicians are likely to buy ELIXIR Strings if their new guitar has our strings installed from the factory. High performance, stellar brand reputation, and a low price are essential to guitar manufacturers. Some might consider guitar manufacturers a marketing partner. Guitar manufacturers buy guitar strings and require ongoing support and services.

Consumers need to be able to purchase your product efficiently, and the channel is an important decision. Too often, there are many options to get your product to market. Not all opportunities are equal. Let's say you invented a new product, and the best way to reach the customer is through retail stores. My experience is that most retailers are not looking to add products to their offerings. It is expensive for them to add a product, and space is limited. Adding your product requires eliminating another product. If you are new to the category, retailers are even more likely to turn you down.

Many inventors rush to present their product ideas to an established company, expect the company to manufacture and sell the product and mail a big royalty check every month. I have sad news for these inventors. Companies are not interested in developing and then selling your product for you. Many companies will refuse to listen to outside ideas to avoid intellectual property disputes. Be careful, inventors. Some companies require you to sign an agreement limiting your product rights if you submit an idea for consideration. Companies are busy inventing and developing their product funnel. The odds of a company developing, manufacturing, and selling your product for you are slim to none.

Direct sales using the Internet offers exceptional opportunities to reach customers early in your product life. Early sales and customer feedback will help you improve your business plan. Amazon makes it simple to sell your product on their site. The challenging part—people need to know why they want your product and where they can buy it. Beware. Products do not sell themselves, and simply placing the product on a website will not lead to success.

Dental hygienists made GLIDE Floss successful. I sampled millions of GLIDE Floss packages to dental professionals and asked them for help. First, let their patients know about the product, and second, ask local retailers to stock the product. You would be surprised how many dental hygienists went to their local stores with information for the retailer to stock GLIDE Floss. Samples to hygienists included a pad of twenty-five small leaflets that explained how retailers could buy

GLIDE Floss. Hygienists would deliver these leaflets to retail store managers.

Early in our launch, I visited the leading drugstore chain during an open-buy day. An open-buy day might be your only chance to meet with a buyer for new products. You arrive when the office opens and sign up for fifteen minutes. Now back to my story.

I arrived for the sales call armed with GLIDE Floss sales data in nearly forty individual stores of this chain. Dental hygienists had convinced local stores to carry the product. The buyer asked to see my list. He read the summary report of sales and reorders, and he was visibly upset. He looked at me and asked, "How is this product in my stores without my permission?" My answer was truthful. I apologized. I explained that I was new to retail, and I had no idea that stores did not have the authority to buy products. I did my best to change the subject to store sales and reorders. Suddenly, the buyer picked up the phone, dialed a number from memory, and asked to speak to a person. I watched the buyer and attempted to overhear the conversation. It turns out he was talking to the manager of one of the stores offering GLIDE Floss. He hung up the phone, repeated his concern with our sales to his stores without permission, visibly relaxed, and then ordered GLIDE Floss for thousands of stores. Proof again that sometimes it is better to seek forgiveness than permission. I did not mean to violate the company policy, but ignorance can work in your favor. Thank you, dental hygienists.

I do not limit my distribution options early in a project. For example, GLIDE Floss in a 200-meter vial, a one-year supply, was available in selected consumer catalogs. Why not? I tried to sell ELIXIR Strings in electronics stores but was unsuccessful.

Once a retailer stocks your product, you own responsibility for the product selling. Celebrate the reorder. Growing sales and reorders are the goals, not distribution. Also, establish monthly reports that allow you to identify retailers who are not reordering products. If reorders are slow, find out why!

The Brand, Logo, and Positioning Statement

Messaging begins with your brand, the logo, and your positioning statement. Coming up with a good brand and logo is challenging. The best products have suggestive names like GLIDE Floss. The problem is most suggestive names are already registered trademarks and are not available. Some companies resort to making up, combining, or misspelling a word as a brand. I have never cared for this, but I am sympathetic to this tactic. I recently purchased a SawStop® job site table saw. SAWSTOP is a registered trademark of SawStop, LLC. The key benefit is the blade stops in contact with skin, and I am much less likely to lose a digit or two. The positioning statement is "Ultimate Safety. Maximum Performance. Ultra-Portable." I like this brand and its positioning. Clear and easily understood.

As noted in the ELIXIR Strings story, we brainstormed names for nine months and searched over 300 possible brands and component brands before settling on ELIXIR Strings featuring POLYWEB Coating. Most people do not know that GLIDE Floss began its life as a component brand, e.g., GLIDE Fiber. Gore intended the fiber to be a component of a branded dental floss sold by a leading oral health care products company. Their name and packaging would feature GLIDE Fiber. Once this strategy failed, I proposed to launch a Gore-branded product called GLIDE Floss. Component branding sounds easy, but good luck with this strategy. Companies buying a product component do not want to promote you or your brand.

Communicating a brand and a component brand is a lot for people to remember, and it takes years to pull off successfully. GORE-TEX apparel is a success story, and it was not easy. As a reminder, Gore sells laminate fabric and seam tape to a company that manufactures clothing at a Gore-approved factory and to Gore specifications. Gore then guarantees the GORE-TEX apparel performance, with the GORE-TEX brand featured on the apparel, including a prominent hangtag. The buying decision for a GORE-TEX jacket is intriguing. The buying decision typically begins with the apparel brand and reputation for style and authenticity. Next, the consumer might insist on GORE-TEX laminate for function and a guarantee. W.L. Gore & Associates guarantees that a jacket featuring GORE-TEX will keep you dry. If your jacket leaks, Gore pays for the repair or refunds the price of the apparel. The following factors in a jacket-buying decision are likely the design, color, fit, and other features like pockets and storage. In "The Barn Coat," I planned to highlight GORE-TEX and WINDSTOPPER fabrics since the selected CONCURVE® brand was unknown. By the way, have you ever heard of a worst lifestyle apparel brand than CONCURVE? That is another story.

I am getting ahead of myself. Let's return to your brand. The brand is one word that you own. It is a promise to the customer that your product will deliver the benefit or benefits you identify. A product with multiple advantages is a blessing and a curse. Suck it up and decide which feature offers the most compelling story. Reinforce this message. One example is ELIXIR Strings. The light coating extends the musical life, but it also reduces the annoying squeak of strings when quickly changing chords. Many musicians experience faster action and comfort depending upon their personal or subjective playing habits. How about:

ELIXIR Strings

Sound Quality That Lasts, Minimal Squeaking, Faster Action, and Comfort!

Too much. Limit your positioning statement to a maximum of six words, preferably a single benefit.

ELIXIR Strings

Sound Quality That Lasts

I was lucky with the GLIDE Floss brand because Bob Gore came up with the GLIDE Fiber component brand, suggesting its benefit. The following was our brand and positioning statement at launch.

GLIDE Floss

Slides Easily Between Teeth Without Shredding

For a while, I used "For People Who Do Not Like to Floss" as the GLIDE Floss positioning statement. It sounds focused, but my guess is 80% of people do not like to floss. Let nylon floss and other fibers have 20% of the market. After a few months, I regained my senses and returned to a benefit positioning statement. Make small mistakes and fix them quickly.

Brand logos and color are essential to the brand's success, and GLIDE Floss featured a comfortable blue logo with a light gray background. The first packaging concepts were bright orange. Not a good look unless it is Halloween or laundry detergent. The GLIDE Floss dispenser was white, and we changed the color of the logo for regular floss, mint-flavored, and tape. Stay with a consistent color scheme to build brand recognition.

ELIXIR Strings packaging was fun. Box color identified the product. Acoustic strings were purple, electric strings were bright blue, bass strings were green, banjo strings were orange, and mandolin strings packaging were blue/green.

Take the time to create a logo style guide and brand guidelines. Rules are essential in making consistent brand messaging and third-party use of your logo. Many companies have dedicated brand managers to build the brand strategy in their marketing function. I am trying to be nice, but I have no idea what a brand manager does? My sense is you can always tell when a company hires a new brand manager because they introduce a new logo in six months and perhaps an updated positioning statement. Updated logos and positioning statements can be helpful, but I am not a fan of routine updates. GLIDE Floss and ELIXIR Strings have new logos and packaging since the launch. I like the new look.

Grassroots Marketing

The concept of grassroots marketing is not hard to understand, but it is challenging to make it work. My version of grassroots and pull marketing goes beyond social media and word-of-mouth. I want to communicate to a targeted group of people who will tell ten people to buy the product. These people must have a credible recommendation.

GLIDE Floss is the ultimate in grassroots marketing. Dental hygienists were the target for about 80% of my marketing investments. The marketing investment was mostly samples and postage. My sister, Priscilla Weaver, was the inspiration for this strategy. She is an exceptional dental hygienist who offered a thorough cleaning with no pain. She is a fierce advocate for daily flossing, and GLIDE Floss was the solution for her patients with tight contacts. Priscilla, and my wife, Pamela, convinced me of the value of GLIDE Floss. I do not use GLIDE Floss and prefer the cheap nylon private-label product. My contacts are not tight, and I have flossed with conventional floss since I was eighteen. My wife did not floss daily until we married. She has close contacts, and flossing can cause snapping of the floss into her gums and shred. Is it any wonder why she prefers GLIDE Floss?

Our dental hygienists' commitment included attending local meetings, booking booths at regional trade shows, and many samples. Samples were strategic. Before attending a trade show, we sent lots of samples to all registered dental hygienists within a zip code. The mailing included an invite to our booth, and we invited their feedback. Some of my best memories are listening to dental hygienists and success stories with patients diligently flossing. By the way, hygienists know if you have only flossed a few days before your cleaning, so do not try to fool them. Clinical trials were persuasive to many dental professionals. Reprints of clinical trials by highly reputable professionals were necessary for our marketing program to work. Some dental professionals were concerned that GLIDE Floss was so good at gliding through tight contacts that it did not disrupt food and plaque between teeth. Reprints of published clinical evaluations and the American Dental Association Seal of Acceptance ended the discussion. Dental hygienists referred hundreds of people to the product, not ten. You cannot get better than this.

One challenge is there are about 150,000 dental hygienists in the United States. Our marketing budget supported sampling to 50,000 dental hygienists just before leading dental trade shows. I reduced the number of hygienists sampled to those located in zip codes relatively close to the event. My experience is you will never have a big enough marketing budget to do everything you want, and just like life, grassroots marketing is all about making smart choices and living within your means.

ELIXIR Strings' grassroots marketing was more complex, and the initial plan identified guitar makers as a compelling pull strategy. Leading guitar brands would feature ELIXIR Strings from the factory, and the musician would naturally buy our product forever. There is just one problem. Guitar makers were not going to install a new, not yet proven brand of strings on their guitars. It was time to pursue Plan B. Plan B was sampling subscribers of leading guitar magazines, beginning with guitar instructors and thousands of musicians who participated in our beta test. We asked the musicians to tell friends and music retailers about the product. It worked but took a lot longer than I had first planned. Once we had credibility, leading guitar manufacturers used our strings as first planned.

I wish I had stories of building strategic alliances to sell CONCURVE® Apparel. Early on, our team investigated strategic alliances with different companies. One of my favorite ideas was a GORE-TEX walking jacket featuring a weight loss company brand. If the member purchased a garment, they could buy a smaller size jacket at a reduced price if they achieved a weight reduction goal. I also tested a cycling jersey sales initiative with a non-profit organization that showed potential. Cause marketing with non-profit companies can be personally gratifying.

Push Marketing

Push marketing is all about product awareness, and I find it easier to execute than grassroots marketing. It includes various activities like websites, brochures, print advertising, trade shows, direct mail, Internet promotions, retailer promotions, and radio or television advertising. Warning! You need lots of cash for effective push marketing.

I am not too fond of push marketing because it is difficult to measure results. How many sales resulted from printing a brochure or a print advertisement? Somehow your push program must focus on product insistence and sales, not just brand awareness.

Trade shows and mailings can be beneficial push marketing activities. However, it takes careful planning and messaging to be successful. Too many companies show up for a trade show, set up a booth, and talk to people who might pass by. Exhibiting at trade shows without prior planning is a waste of time and money. The priority in trade shows is to get your customer to your booth to have an exciting discussion. I exhibited ELIXIR Strings at two trade shows before the launch. The product was called *Gore Experimental Guitar Strings*, with the six guitar strings envelopes packaged in a simple plastic sleeve.

I ran a guitar string print advertisement in two magazines at our second trade show, and the ad is one of my favorites. The ad featured a photomicrograph of our coated string on a calm blue background. The vertical text read "See Something You Have Never Heard Before" and included our booth number. I did not yet have a brand when we created the advertisement. The photomicrograph became a part of our brand messaging in packaging and print advertisements. It is worth mentioning again; you can significantly increase the value of a print advertisement by mailing a color reprint to your customer before the trade show or a sales call.

At product launch, I created a print advertisement for GLIDE Floss directed toward dentists and dental hygienists. The mailing before the trade show included samples and the ad reprint. The ad was just okay, not one of my favorites. The title read "Great Advances in Dental Care" with color photographs of the GLIDE Floss products and black and white pictures of dental artifacts from the National Museum of Dentistry. Beneath the GLIDE Floss picture were four paragraphs of small text that I am certain no one read. I also used the positioning statement "For People Who Do Not Like To Floss." You will not bat a thousand in ad creation. The key learning is to critique any promotional materials objectively and do better next time.

I am a fan of point-of-sale displays and end caps for retailers, appealing packaging, limited advertising, and continued sales calls to retailers to place an order. I use push marketing in support of pull marketing. Push marketing is expensive and challenging to measure. Sales are always the best metric, but it is frequently tricky to tie a deal to a specific activity.

Social Media

Social media is changing how companies can communicate with customers. I say yes to every social media platform, such as Facebook, YouTube, Instagram, and Twitter. However, be careful of messaging apps that suggest instant access. You, and your team, will not likely have time to respond to many messages instantly. On the other hand, many user groups might offer marketing opportunities.

I think social media, like a website, is best for communications and sharing experiences. YouTube is my favorite because I learn visually, and it is always one of my first places to go when I want to learn something quickly.

Social media did not exist when I launched GLIDE Floss. So, the obvious question is, what would I do differently today with social media available? Not much. Our grassroots campaign with dental hygienists relied on personal contact at dental professional events and ongoing sampling products by mail. I would use social media platforms today like the website to communicate product information and news announcements. I would also add social media activity as a specific line item in the twelve-month rolling marketing and sales calendar.

Internet user groups were prevalent when I launched ELIXIR Strings and still are. Beware of user groups. There are multiple guys named "Bob" on these sites that have a mission to spread misinformation. I was lucky because our endorsed artists, like El McMeen and Larry Pattis, were active in the credible guitar music groups. El and others quickly corrected the misinformation, and they had a lot more credibility than Gore in responding to ridiculous claims.

I like LinkedIn. You might be surprised to find how useful LinkedIn is for market research. Employees of companies post surprising details on their site profiles, and you can learn quite a bit by reading these company employee profiles. Do not dedicate your life to LinkedIn research, but it is a tool to discover information.

Social media has become politicized these days, even sites like LinkedIn. My advice is to stay neutral on social media and focus on your product. Taking positions on political issues feels good. But you are likely to tick off 50% of your customers and potential customers in today's world.

Times have changed with sampling programs. In the 1990s, an article in a magazine mentioning free samples would create manageable buzz. Today, multiple websites will publish this offer, and millions of people who could care less about your product will submit a request. It is free. Take care in how you present a proposal for free samples due to broad communication in social media.

A Marketing Success Story

I remember October 8, 1993, like it was yesterday. I was visiting a leading drugstore chain, and its headquarters was only a one-hour drive from my home. The appointment with the buyer was at eight in the morning, and I struggled with this account. I try to make up for less than outstanding sales skills with preparation. So far, my sales pitch had been ineffective, and I did not understand what I needed to do to get the order even after multiple sales calls.

GLIDE Floss was selling well in competitor stores, and I had presented published GLIDE Floss sales reports to demonstrate success as well as a compelling list of new promotional opportunities. My bet was a new products committee was holding up the order, and I needed to provide the buyer with a better internal sales pitch.

At precisely eight in the morning, the buyer walked into the lobby with a big smile on her face. A buyer greeting me in the lobby with a smile was a new experience for me. I was both pleased and confused. She approached me, shook my hand, and said, "Seinfeld."

What?

The Seinfeld show on October 7 featured GLIDE Floss. The episode's title is "The Accountant," and it is a funny episode. Midway through the show, Jerry and Newman are parked in his car while Kramer has gone to a bar to engage with Jerry's financial advisor. The characters suspected the accountant was using drugs, and Kramer was investigating. The scene shifts to Jerry and Newman sitting in the car. Jerry casually looks at Newman and tells him, "You should try this new dental floss called GLIDE." Newman looks dismissively at Jerry and says, "No, I prefer dental tape." The episode then cuts to the bar encounter with Kramer and the accountant, and then back to Jerry's car where Newman is now trying GLIDE Floss. Newman declares he does not like it and still prefers dental tape. Jerry then calls Newman an idiot. The scene ends with Newman placing the used floss on Jerry's dashboard. I was not a regular viewer of Seinfeld at the time, and I had missed the show.

How did GLIDE Floss end up being featured in an episode of the most popular sitcom on television? The answer is luck and an assertive sampling program. In 1993, a short article touting GLIDE Floss appeared in a New York magazine. The report included our toll-free number for a sample. This part of my story may be folklore, but I understand Jerry's real-life mother called Gore and received a GLIDE Floss sample. She liked the product, purchased the 200-meter consumer vials, and gave Jerry the product. The next thing you know, it is featured on a show. Seinfeld featured many products on the show, and I doubt he knows how much he helped make a significant sale to a leading drugstore chain. Our team sent a thank you package to the cast with a range of GLIDE Floss samples and dental tape for the Newman character. The producers sent our team an autographed picture featuring Jerry, George, Elaine, and Kramer. We framed the photograph and displayed it in our office.

We would have eventually secured an order at this retailer, but it would not have been in October 1993. Time is money, so thanks to the Seinfeld show and an assertive marketing campaign for making this happen sooner than later. Luck?

Sales – The Basics

Someday, I would like to launch a product that sells itself. Unfortunately, I doubt this will happen. If you are successful, many people will assume it was easy, and the product sold itself. In the ELIXIR Strings story, I mention a presentation years after the launch claiming our challenge at the trade show launch was writing all the retailers' orders. The reality is that we met with a lot of music retailers but did not make many sales.

Sales begin with understanding your product's value and efficiently communicating this to your customer. Salespeople must focus on the key product benefit. Just explain the product value statement. For example:

GLIDE Floss: Slides Easily Between Teeth Without Shredding

ELIXIR Strings: Sound Quality That Lasts

GORE-TEX Fabrics: Guaranteed To Keep You Dry

WINDSTOPPER Fabrics: Totally Windproof

If interested in the product, the retail buyer will almost immediately jump to pricing and cooperative promotional investments. Do not negotiate the price; it is what it is. Always remember that price is not a number. Price includes terms of sale. Who pays for freight, what is the guarantee, how will the company respond to possible quality issues? Can the retailer return the product for a refund if sales are not robust? Are there stocking fees? Is there a co-op advertising requirement, and does it fit your budget? What is your warranty?

Freight was a challenge when we launched GLIDE Floss. Gore's company policy was the customer pays shipping costs, and our logistics systems did not easily allow Gore to pay the freight. Retailers never pay shipping costs. Their business model requires a fixed number in their Enterprise Resource Planning (ERP) systems to calculate margins. Freight varies by distance. For example, shipping cost from Delaware to Hawaii is higher than shipping costs to Pennsylvania. I completed a comprehensive analysis of the shipping costs of a 24-pack of GLIDE Floss from Delaware to all fifty states. I learned it cost between three cents and five cents a package with Gore-approved shipping companies. I successfully proposed to my leadership to offer GLIDE Floss with or without freight costs. The price difference was ten cents. Every retailer selected the price that included freight. After one year of sales, we discontinued offering the retailer an option to pay transportation costs. The lesson is to do what the customer needs but charge for it. In the GLIDE Floss example, my margins improved, and the customer was okay. Not happy, but okay.

Be proud of your product's value and price. Acknowledge pricing concerns but disagree with this perception. GLIDE Floss wholesale price was three times that of conventional dental floss, and ELIXIR Strings wholesale price was four to five times the price of traditional guitar strings. Retailer pushback on this pricing was fierce. I typically assured the retailer that other professionals had voiced concern with the pricing. Consumers were buying the product at a higher price because the product works. I also provided reference points for price. The cost to use GLIDE Floss once per day was less than four cents. It is not expensive.

Retail point-of-sales data is available for purchase and provides compelling information for a sales call during launch. You can compare your sales to alternative products. After eighteen months or so, GLIDE Floss sales were slowing at our leading retailer. We noticed the sales decline and contacted the buyer to understand the situation better. It was a mystery. This decline made no sense, and it was not consistent with sales at other leading retailers. I engaged a company to visit every store of this retailer and report GLIDE Floss availability. This action cost thousands of dollars, but it was worth the expense. We learned the retailer was not stocking GLIDE Floss at hundreds of stores. We provided a detailed report to the retailer, the buyer placed additional orders to stock stores, and sales grew. The lesson is to track retailer reorder rates. If they lag, investigate and fix the problem.

Once you are a supplier to a retailer, there are two essential requirements. First, product quality must be perfect—no compromising. While learning the retail market, a retail buyer warned me to ensure that every GLIDE Floss package contained at least 50-meters (54.7-yards) as shown on the packaging. His claim is some consumers will unwind the product and measure the contents looking for a "gotcha" moment. The dental floss winding equipment measured the fiber quantity accurately. Just because I am paranoid, I directed the package to include 56-yards of floss and never experienced a quantity claim.

The second retailer requirement is delivery. Terms of sale for leading retailers require you to confirm the order and provide shipping and delivery details. Larger retailers will specify a delivery date and timing window. Finished goods inventory must be sufficient to deliver a large order as soon as the retailer places it. There is good inventory and bad inventory. Finished goods to meet customers' initial demands are essential during the launch, and it is a good inventory. Once established, you can reduce and optimize finished goods inventory to meet ongoing demand.

I am not a fan of exclusive sales arrangements. Retailers and distributors might suggest an exclusive sales agreement to give them an advantage, especially for a compelling new product. I cannot think of a single reason you would want to enter an exclusive selling arrangement. Okay, I have thought of one reason. You are struggling to gain retail distribution, and a key retailer wants a three-month exclusive sales arrangement. I might go for this. The product is available to customers, and you can test grassroots marketing opportunities and direct customers to the retailer. I am stumped to come up with any other scenario that I would consider for exclusive sales deals.

How long is forever? I have confirmed it is one year.

Early in GLIDE Floss's launch, the most prominent dental professional distributor contacted me with a demand. Gore would cease selling our products directly to dental offices, or the distributor would stop selling the product and end our relationship forever. The distributor's sales to dental offices were terrific, so I figured the warning was puffing and said no. Like most distributors, they only offered the top-selling products, not the entire catalog. At this same time, I introduced the option for the dental practice name and number to be printed on our 15-meter patient samples. The distributor had no interest in this program because of the additional processing with no upcharge. Typically, I would charge extra for this service, but the free printing accelerated our consumer sampling program funded by dentists.

I was surprised when the distributor phoned me with their decision to end our relationship forever. I contacted the distributor every few weeks. The buyer did not return my calls. Occasionally I reached the buyer, and he confirmed our relationship was over forever. It is incredible how quickly a year can pass by. Imagine my surprise when we received a stocking order from the distributor through electronic ordering. We filled the order and celebrated the return of a valued customer. Forever is one year.

Respect

You must respect your customers. GLIDE Floss is successful because we communicated directly with dental hygienists, listened to their feedback, and asked for their help in a respectful manner. People like to offer opinions and advice. Jane Gardner and I attended more than one hundred dental hygienist meetings before the launch. We sampled prototype products and asked for feedback. Many hygienists asked about pricing early in our discussions, and these conversations helped us learn the value of our product.

Retail buyers have high-pressure jobs, and I do not envy them. For example, I had a sales call at five in the morning with the buyer for a leading mass merchant retailer. The buyer was working fourteen-hour days.

I made a terrible mistake with a top drugstore buyer while presenting GLIDE Floss. I had visited with the buyer six times and was not making progress in getting a stocking order. In my previous call, she stated she would have to offer the product if two other competitor retailers offered GLIDE Floss. Great! I learned the retailer was a fast follower.

I scheduled an appointment with the buyer shortly after we had orders with the leading retailers. Wow, another big order was coming our way within a few months. In my sales call, I presented the good news to the buyer and reminded her of our understanding. I was excited, not rude. The room began to spin when she immediately listed several new requirements for her to consider stocking GLIDE Floss. Now I screwed up. I was shocked and asked, "Am I spinning my wheels?" She was angry and ended the sales call.

I screwed up, and I still reflect on this mistake. Never vent to the buyer. Retail buyers have a ridiculously tough job and are under significant pressure. Deal with any situation with positive energy, and always show the person respect.

For nine months, I repeatedly called on another retailer, making no progress in getting an order. At this point, you are sure that I am the worst salesperson in the world. I do not want to brag, but I had already sold our product to many drugstore chains and mass merchants. "I just want it all." Now back to my retailer story. After months of sales calls, I received a call from the buyer. She was angry and asked me a simple question, "How can you have sold GLIDE Floss into four leading drugstore retailers and not to our stores?" Just a reminder, I had visited the buyer multiple times and made my best sales pitch.

What is the correct answer?

It took me five seconds, but I answered correctly. I figured out that the buyer was in trouble with her boss for not stocking GLIDE Floss sooner. My answer was, "I made a mistake, and I am sorry. I am new to retail and learning every day. I will be on a flight tomorrow to visit with you, review a proposed order, and commit to promotional opportunities. Please let your management know that I am sorry." The buyer told me she would contact me after she spoke to her boss. I met with the buyer the next day, she placed an order that week, and sales exceeded expectations. This story had a happy ending, and I respected the buyer. On the flight to visit the retailer, I thought about an alternative answer. Like, "Are you crazy. I have been calling on you for nine months. We have spoken a dozen times. You had the opportunity to be the first large retailer chain offering the product. Are you crazy?" No, this is not the correct answer. Do not pick a fight with a customer, and you can vent when driving alone in the rental car to the appointment.

I worked with a product manager for years, and he had a sign in his office that read, "Salesman Wanted. Must Look Honest." Customers can easily spot a lazy or unethical salesperson. A dental hygienist, Janifer Brown, was the second salesperson we hired in GLIDE Floss and a natural leader. Located in Seattle, she managed large accounts west of the Mississippi. I remember traveling with her to large retailers, and she not only looked honest, but her customers knew they could trust her. She had a fantastic ability to strike up a conversation with any buyer and the ability to listen actively. Janifer also asked great questions so that she understood the customer's perspective. The challenge in sales is to balance advocacy for the customer and loyalty to your company. It comes down to judgment. You can teach it, but sometimes people just do not get it.

A trait of a successful salesperson is listening. Early in the GLIDE Floss launch, Jane Gardner and I participated in a unique retailer tradeshow. We paid a fee, and we were guaranteed to talk with twenty-five relevant retailers. The organizers arranged one hundred retailers at a five-foot table in a large hotel ballroom. Typically, two representatives were there from the company. A bell would ring, and you would have one minute to walk to your appointment. The appointment was for two minutes. Jane and I prepared a two-minute sales pitch that we thought was compelling. It was not. We quickly learned that you discover nothing about the retailer if you talk for two minutes. So, we changed our sales pitch to under thirty seconds and spent ninety seconds asking questions and listening. This trade show was one of the best training events of my life.

A final reminder in respecting your customer is to prepare for the sales call. Never wing it. If you are lucky enough to get a leading retailer's time, you should plan on no more than fifteen minutes. Assume pleasantries will take a few minutes. Make your sales pitch in a few minutes. The remainder of the time is active listening. Active listening is asking questions and listening to the answers. I participated in moot court competitions in law school. It is an exciting competition where teams simulate appellate court oral arguments. Law school professors act as appellate judges, and you must argue both sides of the case. The key to success in the moot court competition is preparation, listening to questions, and being quick on your feet. Perhaps salespeople should participate in a moot court competition for training. It is no different.

Know Your Product

A good salesperson knows the product and is an excellent business person. They celebrate the first order but measure their reorders and sustainable sales success. GLIDE Floss and ELIXIR Strings had a lot of SKUs. Salespeople must understand which SKUs are more likely to sell in a particular retailer. For example, drugstore chains are more likely to offer a range of dental floss, including tape, floss holders, picks, and single-use sachets. Grocery stores will likely provide one SKU to their customers. For GLIDE Floss, this would be the mint-flavored 50-meter. If the buyer selects unflavored floss, the salesperson will tap the buyer on the shoulder and suggest flavored floss.

Carolyn Harrell was the first product specialist for ELIXIR Strings. Her first project was to create a sales training binder and present it to the salespeople. The first section offered details from the business plan relevant to sales. The technology section was not limited to a coated string. Carolyn began the training with "What is sound?" Next, she explained wave technology such as wavelength, amplitude, period, and frequency. Next, guitar string construction was detailed so that salespeople could discuss the core wire, wrap wire, the ball end, and string materials for a range of guitars, mandolins, and banjos. Carolyn was a mechanical engineer, and she enjoyed teaching. Her efforts allowed our salespeople to be teachers. This training resulted in our team being better than the competition. I bet that most experienced guitar players do not understand the physics of waves. The training materials' final section was marketing details, including ad reprints for distribution to buyers. A similar training manual would have helped salespeople in the GLIDE Floss team, especially new hires.

Knowledge of the product goes far beyond product and SKU details. To be an influential advisor to the customer, the salesperson must be an expert in fulfillment, processing capabilities like EDI, invoicing practices, terms of sale, and return protocol. Sales professionals must also understand the legal issues that can cause significant problems. Antitrust and fair competition are examples. Training in these topics should be crystal clear, with no room for error. A best practice is never talking with the competition. Nothing good can come from these conversations. Also, certain words and phrases must be avoided, even in jest. Examples are "dominating the market" and "crushing the competition." These phrases imply you are engaged in antitrust activities.

Knowledge of the product and terms of sale enables a great salesperson to provide early warnings of problems with the market, a customer, or the product. A key to managing problems is effective communication and full disclosure. If I make a mistake, I inform every person impacted, apologize profusely, and explain what I have learned to avoid future problems. The customer will not be happy but will be grateful for the information. An example is late delivery. If the buyer discovers this mistake from their organization, they will be upset with you. There is a good chance the buyer will forgive the error if the salesperson explains the situation to the buyer as soon as possible with a corrective action plan. No surprises must be the standard.

Hiring Your Sales Team

Never delegate marketing and sales if you are leading the product launch. You own the customer interface. I have trusted others to oversee finance, supply chain, logistics, manufacturing, engineering, and product development to make more time for marketing and sales.

Hiring a new sales team is a blast. It can also be the difference between success and failure. I have been successful with unconventional hiring. In GLIDE Floss, my first five sales hires were dental hygienists responsible for professional and retailer sales. They immediately impacted dental professional marketing and sales but started at ground zero in retail sales. Dental hygienists are intelligent, personable, and enjoy being with people. Experienced salespeople might have been intimidated by the relatively high price of GLIDE Floss. However, dental hygienists believe in the product's value and are proud of the product offering.

I contracted with my sister Priscilla, a dental hygienist, to work dental shows and witnessed her selling ability. The first GLIDE Floss hire, Jane Gardner, was willing to do any job to meet customer expectations. One of my favorite memories is Jane Gardner traveling to dental professional meetings and scheduled retailer calls for the entire month of July. Jane checked her luggage when traveling from a dental show to the Midwest for a retailer sales call. Oops. She arrived late in the day without her luggage. Her appointment was at eight in the morning the following day, and she had traveled in shorts, flip-flops, and a T-shirt. What do you do? Jane arrived for the sales call dressed in shorts, flip-flops, and a T-shirt with a sincere apology. The buyer enjoyed the conversation with Jane, and she got the order. Jane demonstrated excellent judgment and learned to carry on an emergency change of clothes on future trips. Or maybe she should have conducted future sales calls in shorts and a T-shirt? Just kidding.

I recruited Jane Gardner to take the lead in ELIXIR Guitar Strings sales. Neither Jane nor I play the guitar. We have a picture of the two of us at a NAMM trade show holding guitars, and it is remarkable music retailers even stopped to talk with us. We knew the guitar string market, our product, and retail sales, so we were okay. Jane confirmed that we did not need to hire musicians to sell guitar strings. One exception was Michael Lille. Check Michael out at michaellillemusic.com. I met Michael at the Kerrville Folk Festival, where he was a performing musician. Michael is a natural listener and an exceptional musician and songwriter. He likes and respects people. I offered Michael the opportunity to visit music retailers representing ELIXIR Strings as an independent contractor. It was amazing. Wherever Michael traveled, orders followed. We quickly hired Michael as a full-time marketing and salesperson, and we accommodated his music commitments. Michael was also vital in upgrading our artist relations program. I also contracted with several musicians to work the NAMM trade show at the ELIXIR Strings launch. Thank you, Larry Pattis and Michael Camp. Both musicians provided retailers credible ELIXIR String testimonials.

There are three lessons I have learned in hiring sales professionals. First, always hire people more intelligent than you. Second, seek diversity in the team. Third, provide high-impact training and sales objectives. Then, let the sales team do their job.

Lesson 4. Marketing and Sales Lessons

- Create an integrated grassroots marketing and sales plan with a rolling twelve-month visual map of marketing activities and how they relate to sales activities.

- Develop a thorough knowledge of your market, market segments, and customer needs.

- Develop a grassroots pull marketing strategy supported by limited push marketing activities.

- Know your product inside and out. If you do not believe in the value, then your customer will not believe in the product.

- Respect your customer, and never vent to them. Take ownership of any problems. Do not be defensive and if your product is sold in retail stores, help your buyer win.

- Products do not sell themselves; hire intelligent, passionate, and customer-focused salespeople.

Lesson 5. Leadership and Teams

Inspirational Leaders

How many inspirational leaders have you met, or better, have you worked for an inspirational leader? I only know a handful of extraordinary leaders in my career so far. There are not that many great leaders. Leadership is a hot topic, with more articles and books than just about any other business subject. The challenge is leadership is not a formula or something that you learn after reading a book or attending a seminar. Being a good leader requires self-awareness, hard work, and practice.

Years ago, I witnessed the worst example of business leadership. One of the Gore division leaders called a meeting with three hundred or so Associates to discuss division morale. Morale was bad. He booked an auditorium at the University of Northern Arizona in Flagstaff. I had high hopes for the meeting, and it was an opportunity for the division leader to state a problem, invite feedback, and listen. Good leaders have an uncanny ability to observe, listen, and learn. By definition, a Gore leader is a person who has followers. This Gore leader opened the meeting by speaking behind a large podium that seemed to be a barrier between him and the audience. The Associate began the discussion by observing people were not happy. Acknowledging an issue is an excellent start to the meeting. Rather than discussing morale, the person announced the division's problem was not leadership but followership—what a unique twist on the Gore definition of a leader. We were all lousy followers. I do not remember the rest of the meeting, but I did get a good laugh from the claim of being an imperfect follower. Morale did not improve because of this meeting.

You cannot control whether you work for a good leader. My advice is to be self-aware, manage your weaknesses, and work hard to be an extraordinary leader. You can control this.

Leader – Defined

There are millions of managers, but my experience is that less than half of these managers are leaders. Moreover, many managers lack self-awareness and empathy. The worst managers are narcissists.

I have six requirements to be a leader:

- Smart

- Strategic

- Good Judgment

- Accountable

- Learner

- Honest

The first attribute is to be smart, and this goes far beyond intelligence. My peers at the Naval Academy, law school, the US Navy, DuPont, Gore, and Eaton with the highest IQ were not always the best leaders. I had a friend in the Engineering Department at DuPont that was struggling. I was in the Power Services Division, an internal engineering consultant organization for DuPont manufacturing plants. It was a challenging environment. You had one year to build relationships and financial commitments from DuPont manufacturing plants to support your salary and overhead. After nine months in the division, my friend asked me why he was failing? I was constructive, and I explained he was too smart for his own good. He likely had the highest IQ in our group. If asked, what is 2 + 2, he could not say 4. Instead, he would want to talk about the theory of addition. He might submit a proposal to a plant to optimize an industrial refrigeration system. The local engineer who would sell the project to plant management would ask for the project's critical benefit. My friend might then spend fifteen minutes explaining the refrigeration cycle and mention the project's outcome in passing. The correct answer is that optimizing the refrigeration unit condenser pressure by the year's season will result in documented electrical savings of $50,000 in the next year with a project cost of $10,000. Then, stop talking.

The second attribute of a leader is to be strategic. A strategic leader sees the big picture in a tricky business and technology environment. It is easier to be strategic when things are going well than in challenging times. Being strategic requires the ability to lay out a vision for the future. Being a visionary is also a lot harder than it sounds. Many managers believe their job is to protect what exists rather than grow the business. My friend Dave Myers says it is safer for a manager to say "no" than "yes." There is no power in "yes." A disruptive plan can fail, and many managers believe failure is too high a personal risk. I think risk-averse managers destroy more businesses than competition or market conditions by saying "no."

Good judgment is the next attribute of a leader. Justice Potter Stewart had a famous phrase in a 1964 opinion, Jacobellis v. Ohio, 378 US 184 (1964), to describe a somewhat vague threshold test for obscenity. "I know it when I see it..." Well, I know good judgment when I see it. Leaders thoroughly evaluate a situation and weigh the alternatives' strengths and weaknesses, even under tremendous pressure. They also work with a team to implement solutions. A leader welcomes diversity in a group and has the good sense to listen to alternative views. They recruit intelligent people to join the organization, and many leaders claim to be a "talent hawk." Every person has a bias and weaknesses. Some managers are a victim of their success. I like a new environment where I do not know what I am doing. A new environment can be a product, a market, or a function. I am much more open to new ideas when I am clueless. Once I know how to do something, I tend to repeat the same solution to a challenge. Knowledge and experience can be a weakness and compromise judgment. Be careful.

Law school helped me to think more strategically. University of Maryland Law School used the Socratic learning method when I was a student. I still remember my first class, Contracts, with Professor Scott Reynolds. Professor Reynolds was brilliant and an expert in the Socratic learning method, and he began the first class with a simple question. An actress is a guest on a late-night talk show and states, "I will give $50,000 to the person who can tell me how to lose weight and to keep it off." An audience member stands and says, "Regular exercise and a good diet will result in sustainable weight loss." Does the actress owe the audience member $50,000? Professor

Reynolds used the Socratic method to delve into a contract's elements, making persuasive points that suggested a $50,000 payment might be appropriate. The answer is relatively easy, and no payment is due since the actress did not intend to bind herself in a contract. The Socratic teaching method is like "Critical Thinking Skills" that are popular in business today. Thinking and assessing the situation objectively leads to the right decisions and a reputation for sound judgment.

My next attribute of a leader is accountability. My experience is that many managers have developed a skill never to be accountable, so many managers are not leaders. One of four principles at W.L. Gore & Associates is "commitment," defined as a person making their commitments and keeps them. Accountability begins with making a commitment and taking responsibility for decisions and failures. Accountability was a key strength of Ritchie Snyder, which I will discuss in the next section. Ritchie kept his commitments and was exceptionally skilled in holding himself and others responsible. My style with Ritchie was to be an open book. Ritchie was the first to know the error and the corrective action plan if I made a mistake.

I remember a GLIDE Floss packaging mistake I made early in the project. I ordered boxes to hold twelve GLIDE Floss dental professional prototype samples. I used the boxes to distribute samples to dental hygienists at local events in Delaware, Maryland, and Pennsylvania. Printed in a small font beneath the GLIDE Floss logo was "GLIDE is a registered trademark of W.L. Gore Associates, Inc." Ritchie flipped out when I showed him the box and my mistake. Ritchie forcefully reminded me of the importance of printed materials being accurate with no errors. Do you see my mistake? I am missing the ampersand (e.g., "&") between Gore and Associates. Ritchie concluded the discussion with a demand that I present him with a plan to avoid future mistakes. I had a plan already summarized that called for three credible people to review any printed materials before sign-off and production. Ritchie was okay with this solution, and it is a best practice. I have previously mentioned that the definition of a best practice is how I like to do it.

A leader enjoys learning. Learning begins with curiosity. Dave Myers, the inventor of ELIXIR Strings, is the most curious person I have met, and Dave is an inspirational leader. A leader is also a good teacher and enjoys watching others learn and succeed. A learner likes new situations and actively seeks new ways to grow. A learner reads books and professional materials. I carry three reading materials when I travel, including a business book, a professional journal, and a novel. I read the novel in the evening when my concentration is lower, and I enjoy a legal thriller. My experience is many managers do not read and are not curious.

Learning is attitude. I was a good memorizer in high school and college, which served me well for exams. Memorization is not learning because you quickly forget what you memorized. I learned this when I joined the DuPont Engineering Department. On several occasions, I had studied the Rankine thermodynamic cycle in the Navy, and it was a question in my interviews for the DuPont job. I remembered enough for the interview, but I became a Rankine cycle student when I arrived at DuPont and worked as a consultant in the Power Services Division. Law school was the first time I tried to learn in school versus memorize. Being a learner results in you being more adaptable and open-minded. Some experts can be frightening and have stopped learning. These experts offer a valued opinion based on their collection of knowledge. I launched GLIDE Floss in Gore because the experts at the leading oral health care companies knew it was only worth a slight premium over conventional nylon dental floss. The experts were wrong and prevented GLIDE Floss's launch for twenty years. The experts had stopped learning. Leaders need to continue learning and be open to new ideas.

A leader must have integrity and be honest. Honesty begins with the company you start or where you work. I am lucky because I never doubted the US Navy, DuPont, Gore, or Eaton's commitment to ethics. Honesty was a core value of all these organizations, and it is the leader who makes ethics and integrity a way of life. The leader is a role model for ethical decision-making and consistently reinforces expectations for honest behavior. I joined Eaton when Sandy Cutler was the Chairman and Chief Executive Officer. Sandy is a great leader, and he was committed to creating an atmosphere of truthfulness. I do not know if you can teach ethics, but Eaton requires annual ethics training, and it is a clear reminder to all employees of the importance of integrity. My first memory of being troubled by ethics was my plebe year at the Naval Academy. My roommate and I studied for our first semester exams when he suddenly commented that he might cheat in an examination the next day. I was shocked since cheating and honesty are the foundation of training at the Naval Academy.

I told him to knock it off, and I would report him if I knew he cheated. The next day he was caught cheating in an examination and was dismissed from the Naval Academy. I often wonder whether he was dishonest or just wanted to figure out how to leave the Naval Academy without resigning? My bet is he was unhappy and preferred to leave the Academy. Maybe being released was more acceptable than quitting? I do not know.

I enjoy working for people who are intelligent, strategic, have good judgment, accountable, learners, and honest. Who would not? Leaders get results, and I think it is because of these attributes. I am proud to be an Eagle Boy Scout. While writing this recap, my leadership attributes are like the twelve principles a Boy Scout lives by, including "trustworthy, loyal, helpful, friendly, courteous, kind, obedient, cheerful, thrifty, brave, clean, and reverent." Let us include the Boy Scout Motto, "Be Prepared," as a leadership lesson.

A few random thoughts. Leaders have a sense of humor and can laugh at themselves. Always be positive and consistent. Do not play favorites with team members. Playing favorites will destroy a team. Always lead by example. Praise in public, and only criticize in private. Make reasonable accommodations for team members' schedules and treat people like adults. Good leaders are selfless and share the credit for success. Set high expectations, and do not micro-manage. When I was a Lieutenant Commander in the Naval Reserve, I had a new boss who started the weekend drill with a priorities meeting. I had several big projects underway, left the priorities meeting to check in with my team, and settled in for a day's work. Within thirty minutes, my new boss came to my office and asked, "How are you doing on your assignments?" I behaved myself and respectfully explained I was just getting started and would like to update him later that morning. You get one chance to make a first impression. My first impression of my new Commanding Officer was that of a micromanager. But I learned that he was a good leader after just a few weekends. Maybe he was a bit too anxious the first weekend of command? Finally, recognize people on your team. It does not have to be big; perhaps just a sincere thank you every so often.

Again, I think most managers today are not leaders. How do so many managers get promoted to leadership positions in an organization, yet they are not leaders? I have worked for several idiots. These managers are innovative and strategic, but they generally lack good judgment, hide from accountability, and are not learners. They have a unique skill, the exceptional ability to "manage up," and they couldn't care less about their peers or people who report to them. Managing up includes the ability to always be in the room to take credit for results, avoid accountability, and have an uncanny aptitude to say the right thing at the right time. Some leaders perceive these people as high talent only because of their ability to "manage up." They have one priority—their success. That is it. I have no use for these managers, and they will never be leaders. The good news is poor performance or situational challenges eventually catch up with these managers. But do not be disappointed. Some of these managers survive for an entire career.

Finally, lighten up. Leaders are not perfect. Leaders have bad days and can be distracted by stress with work, family, health, or a hundred other challenges. Leaders also make mistakes. I like the argument that there are no bad decisions, just bad outcomes. You make the best decision you can with the data available. If you are fortunate enough to work with a leader, let them have ups and downs, just like any person.

Inspirational Leaders – Examples

So far, I have worked for about a dozen people in my career. Most were excellent managers or good leaders, but only two were inspirational leaders. Maybe I need to get out more often, but there are just not many leaders who inspire me. I will discuss Ritchie Snyder and Bob Gore, two inspirational leaders I worked with during the GLIDE Floss and ELIXIR Strings launch. I did not work for Bob Gore, so I include a discussion of Mark McGuire. Mark is an inspirational leader who led the Law Department at Eaton.

Ritchie A. Snyder

I had the privilege of working for Ritchie Snyder for eleven years at W.L. Gore & Associates. Ritchie was my sponsor, which means he was my coach, advocate, and friend. Ritchie passed away in 2002, and he was only fifty-four years old. Ritchie joined W.L. Gore & Associates after earning a bachelor's degree in engineering from the University of Delaware.

Ritchie was an extraordinary leader, and I think of Ritchie almost every day. The usual context is the question, "What would Ritchie do?" So, what is unique about Ritchie that makes him a remarkable leader? First, he was an outstanding manager. Second, Ritchie was brilliant, strategic, had exceptional judgment, was accountable, a learner, and honest to the core. He had two additional attributes that made him an inspirational leader to me:

- Loyalty

- Respect

My version of loyalty is "having my back." I could trust Ritchie to hold me accountable and to help me learn. My conversations and opinions were private, and I know Ritchie was an objective advocate for me to Gore's leadership.

Loyalty does not mean loyal no matter what. You may recall that Ritchie fired me from the GLIDE Floss team. Being fired was not warranted, but sometimes life is not fair. Ritchie provided me and my wife assurances that all would be well for me at Gore. Ritchie was pragmatic and knew when to fight a battle. Loyalty is a two-way street, and it only works when the leader and the follower trust each other. Ritchie was an incredible coach. He hired me to start a business with zero product and general management experience. He took a bet on me, and it paid off. Hiring me was a risk that only an authentic leader would take.

The second attribute of an extraordinary leader is respect. Gore Associates respected Ritchie because he was a proven business executive. His business strategy, product development, marketing, and pricing skills resulted in business success. Ritchie was not shy in offering his opinion. I traveled with Ritchie a few months after he became my sponsor to a leading oral health care company's headquarters to meet with senior executives to confirm they were not interested in adding GLIDE Floss to their product portfolio. I wish I had a video of the meeting. We met for about forty-five minutes, and Ritchie owned the room. He engaged with fun and exciting stories, offered Gore company history, and sold the benefits of floss made with GLIDE Fiber. It was the ultimate sales call, even though we did not get the order. Their experts claimed that our value pricing assumptions were wrong, and the product had unacceptable margins. The low-price premium for GLIDE Fiber was a safe story for managers. Still, Ritchie had earned the respect of every attendee of that meeting in just forty-five minutes.

Respect works two ways, and Ritchie respected me. He knew my weaknesses but focused more on my strengths. Ritchie never tried to "fix me." Ritchie was demanding but never unreasonable. He treated me and others the way that he wanted to be treated. Ritchie challenged me to be a better person, and he took joy in my success. Ritchie frequently asked two questions, "What do you think?" and "How can I help you?" He had a poster in his office that read:

Good Judgment

Comes From Experience.

Experience Comes From

Bad Judgment.

Mark Twain has a quote that may have been the source for this poster. Twain said, "Good decisions come from experience. Experience comes from making bad decisions."

Ritchie did not encourage mistakes, but he allowed you to make a mistake if you learned from it. His leadership helped guide my team and me to achieve our goals. I have heard people claim there are two types of leaders, those that give you energy and those that take your energy. I do not buy this. Leaders inspire people and provide them with energy, and Ritchie was an incredible energy source. Managers take your energy.

My life is better because I worked for Ritchie Snyder.

Robert "Bob" W. Gore

I joined W.L. Gore & Associates in Newark, Delaware, as an engineer in a startup polymers facility. Gore leased a warehouse and hired a small team to build a pilot manufacturing capability for a new line of innovative solvent-free adhesives for company products. The new adhesives were consistent with the Gore story of technology, high performance, a better environment, and employee safety. In addition, the adhesives' inventions and development were exceptional innovations by a team of talented Gore chemists.

Shortly after arriving at Gore, I attended the last hour of a global leadership meeting to listen to the wrap-up presentation by Bob Gore. Bob was the Chairman and President of Gore at the time. His presentation was on the Paper Mill East facility's second floor, a former manufacturing plant used for corporate activities. In the room was a large banner hanging from the ceiling. It declared, "**MAKE MONEY NOW!**" Bob drove this message hard in his conclusion, and I still recall this message in any new project or activity I pursue. "Make Money Now!" is a perfect positioning statement. Three words that scream passion, with or without an exclamation point. Focus is critical, and there was no doubt of what Bob was demanding of his broader leadership team—they were to make money. You cannot be any more urgent than "now."

Authentic leaders are passionate, and genuine passion is infectious. People want to be a member of a successful and exciting organization. Passion is not about being a cheerleader. It is about caring and making a difference with exceptional products or services, making money, creating jobs, and improving the environment. I believe that most managers who are cheerleaders in the work environment are phony, and I imagine them sticking pins into a voodoo doll late in the evenings screaming, "Serenity now!" Cheerleaders are almost always managers who do not know how to lead people. Cheerleaders are terrible at launching new products. "Yea, Team!"

Urgency is not about setting unrealistic timelines or creating a crisis environment. Speed is about understanding priorities, focusing on tasks at hand, and delivering on commitments. Every team member must understand their unique role in making the business and their team successful. If you do not know how you fit, it is just a job. Some people procrastinate. If I do not get this done today, then definitely tomorrow. If not tomorrow, maybe by the end of the week. I know these people, and they can destroy a team. Procrastinators should not launch new products.

For me, "Make Money Now" is both a leadership and marketing lesson. Three words say it all and have inspired me to focus on why a corporation employs me. Bob was hands-on, especially with brands. He came up with the GLIDE brand and reviewed and approved the ELIXIR brand. I asked Bob to join the critical reviews for GLIDE Floss and ELXIR Strings, and he never missed a meeting.

I did not capture Bob Gore's attention day-to-day. He was a busy guy as Chairman and President of the Gore company. He was an inspirational leader, demanding but respectful, and loyal when I needed his help. Bob is the most intelligent person I have met, and I am not exaggerating. Ritchie and Bob had different leadership styles, but both are inspirational, and I try to emulate them. Bob Gore passed away on September 17, 2020, and thousands of people he helped miss him.

Mark M. McGuire

Mark McGuire was the Executive Vice President and General Counsel for Eaton from 2005 until he retired in 2017. Eaton is a diversified industrial company that sells electrical, aerospace, hydraulics, automotive, truck, and filtration products. Sales in 2020 were $17.9B with about 90,000 employees. Eaton is a big company. I know many attorneys, and Mark McGuire is the best attorney I have met. He is brilliant, strategic, decisive, builds teams, challenges people to learn, and is committed to continuous improvement.

I worked for Mark from 2011 to 2017, and I knew from day one that he was an inspirational leader. In 2010, Eaton became aware of a US government contracts compliance issue that signaled a need for improved controls. Mark proposed to create a new Government Contracts Compliance organization in the Law Department. Mark was a problem-solver and recognized the critical need to comply with complicated government accounting and other regulations fully. Eaton has considerable revenue from government contracts that were at risk. Mark is accountable and raised his hand to take the lead.

My name was floated to build a new Government Contracts specialty practice group (SPG) in the Law Department. Mark made inquiries about me, and he decided I was a good candidate for the job. At the time, I led Business Development in the Industrial Sector, and I did not know anything about government contracts. But Mark was willing to take a bet that I could learn this practice area. My interview with Mark for the job was friendly. I confirmed I had passed the Maryland and Pennsylvania bar examinations, and my law license was active in both states. Mark advised me to immediately make an application to be admitted as corporate counsel in Ohio. My first action was to immerse myself in government contracts and to build a compliance organization. Mark gave his okay for me to engage with Tom Lemmer, a partner in the McKenna Long & Aldridge LLP's Denver office, for an in-person full day of questions. US government contracts are remarkably complex. Only two lawyers are experts in the field, and they do not agree with each other (a joke). But Tom Lemmer is one of a handful of experts in government contracts, and I wanted to build a learning foundation with his expertise. Without hesitation, Mark approved the investment and encouraged me to learn.

Mark consistently challenged me with new opportunities, and this is a trait of an inspirational leader. I led the Law Department's annual governance review, a three-hour staff meeting to assess the Law Department's organization and performance. It was remarkable how this meeting drove innovation and a commitment to improving the Law Department's value.

Mark also encouraged me to lead the annual Law Department strategic planning process, and I always began the first strategic planning meeting with a SWOT analysis. The lawyers leading SPGs at Eaton are exceptional. They are very bright and determined to grow and learn. The SWOT session was always interesting, and SWOT had a significant impact on my career. In 2012, the leadership team identified global contracts as a weakness. Contracts were not centralized, and it was inefficient. High-priced business and IP attorneys managed simple NDAs. Businesses had contract employees reporting to customer service, sales, or finance. Improving global contracts became a strategic focus for the Law Department, and Mark asked me and a sector business attorney to lead a process to improve contracts at Eaton. Two years later, I became Vice President and Chief Counsel, Global Contracts, increasing my responsibilities. Thank you, Mark!

I could always count on Mark to coach me. For example, he helped me better assess the implications of legal issues and which problems leadership needed briefings. For instance, after joining the Law Department, I tended to overcommunicate problems. Overcommunication might sound good, but it is distracting in a large business.

I am grateful to have worked for Mark McGuire. I am a better problem-solver, leader, and lawyer because of his skills in delegation and coaching.

Self-Awareness

If your boss is a lousy leader, accept it, and do your best. However, do not dwell on the leadership skills of your boss. Instead, learn how to work with your boss even if they are an average manager.

Never forget you have complete control over your leadership style, and it is essential to work every day to be an inspirational leader. It is a high bar, but wouldn't it be great if there were more leaders? I have not reached this bar, but I continue to strive to be an extraordinary leader.

I have earned a mixed reputation as a leader. My passion, urgency, and drive for results can be challenging for people who prefer a less dynamic work environment. I have high expectations for myself and my colleagues. Mistakes are okay if we learn from them. Transparency and ethical behavior are a must. No secrets. I have no time for idiots or foolish behavior. I know that I am far from perfect, but my intentions are good. My leadership style, like Ritchie Snyder, can be intimidating. I do not try to fix these traits. It is who I am.

I am impatient. Impatience happens when my sense of urgency goes too far, and I have set unreasonable goals. I do my best to manage this trait. I can be judgmental. I have strong opinions, and my style might suggest I am not open-minded. I also do my best to manage this trait. I have learned that I like an active discussion that some might consider an argument. Disagreement does not bother me. State your case, and I will try to change your opinion if I disagree. I have learned most people do not enjoy a volatile discussion, and I try to avoid conflict.

I am situationally disruptive. GLIDE Floss and ELIXIR Strings demanded significant internal and external disruption to be successful. I left Gore to join Eaton to lead Business Development in the Industrial Sector. It is a great job, including supporting business strategy development, building an acquisition pipeline, and drafting executives' presentations. I had to learn PowerPoint quickly; I was more of a Word guy when I arrived. The job was challenging but not disruptive. My leadership style also changed when I joined Eaton. It is a larger company with a more established process and protocol. Eaton is a great company but different from Gore. My transfer to the Law Department required me to be disruptive again. The bottom line is leadership can be situational. You must be self-aware and adapt.

If you are launching a new product, be a disruptive leader. A key question is, are you self-aware of your leadership style and the weaknesses you need to manage?

The Team

Teams are popular today, or at least the idea of teams. Teams are not complicated. It is a group of people who have individual skills working together for a common goal.

Unfortunately, many people are called a team but do not share a common goal or have the range of skills necessary for success.

A story attributed to Abraham Lincoln comes to mind.

Question: How many legs would a dog have if we call the dog's tail a leg?

Easy Answer: Five.

Response: No, the answer is four. Calling a dog's tail a leg does not make it a leg.

Calling a group of people a team does not make them a team. The story of ELIXIR Strings is all about a great team. A group of exceptional people did not just happen. Dave Myers and I recruited people with specific skills to solve problems. Dave Myers had the idea of an improved guitar string and was hands-on in technology, manufacturing, quality, and business plan reviews. Glenn Bethke is a guitar strings co-inventor, an expert in films, and he developed new technology. Joe Huppenthal is a guitar strings co-inventor, an expert in manufacturing processes, and he methodically developed a coating process that resulted in great sound and durability. Glenn and Joe did not work in silos. They worked together with Dave Myers, Chuck Hebestreit, Patti Prescott, Ann Stump, Jeannie Guthrie, Jane Gardner, and me. I am not a big fan of meetings, but we did assemble the group weekly to summarize issues and next steps. We shared a passion for making the first coated guitar string that musicians would favor over conventional guitar strings. But for a team effort, ELIXIR Guitar Strings would not exist. It would just be another idea. It took nine months, but our team came up with the brand ELIXIR Strings featuring POLYWEB Coating. Brainstorming brands was great fun.

I am proud of the team I built to manufacture and sell GLIDE Floss. I had worked alone far too long in developing the GLIDE Floss product specifications, business planning, manufacturing process, FDA regulations, independent product testing, dispenser design, and one hundred plus other tasks. I had a lot of help, but there was no team, just me. My health suffered, and it was not as fun as it should have been. The project became more fun as the team came together. The first hire was Jane Gardner to lead sales and marketing. Jane was a recent graduate of the University of Maryland's dental hygiene program, and she was a perfect hire. A natural salesperson, she worked on any task necessary for the project's success. My key learning from GLIDE Floss was to never work alone in the launch of a new product. I know I need to work in a small team.

A misconception with teams is they have a single leader, and all others are team members. Leadership is situational in the best teams. Yes, I know there will be one person who might be the team's face. A good leader knows when to take the lead or take a step back and allow another team member to take charge. For example, Jeannie Guthrie led finance and manufacturing for ELIXIR Strings. Jane Gardner and Janifer Brown led sales in GLIDE Floss. John Dolan led technology in GLIDE Floss, and Dave Myers led technology in ELIXIR Strings. I am not using "led" casually in these examples. These people are all great leaders and exceptional teammates.

The Ultimate Team – USS Skipjack (SSN 585)

I served aboard the USS *Skipjack* (SSN 585) for forty-two months as a nuclear-trained Submarine Warfare Officer. The *Skipjack* was a fast attack submarine based out of Groton, Connecticut, the first in its class featuring a high-speed hull design and an S5W nuclear reactor. The *Skipjack* is relatively small compared to the latest attack submarines, 252 feet long compared to 377 feet long for the new Virginia class subs. *Skipjack* had about 100 crew members, ten to twelve officers, and about ninety enlisted personnel. A submarine joke is "SSN" stands for "Saturdays, Sundays, and nights." If you enjoy a demanding environment, you are an excellent candidate to serve on a nuclear submarine.

In nuclear power training, junior officers training for nuclear ship roles submit a request for their preferred ship type and port location. I requested a Los Angeles class submarine based in Hawaii or San Diego. Los Angeles class submarines were the newest and most capable fast-attack subs at the time. So, it was no surprise when the powers that be at the Pentagon assigned me to one of the oldest submarines in service in Connecticut. I believe in fate, and I am thankful every day for this assignment because my future wife's brother was a shipmate on the *Skipjack*. I would not have met Pamela but for being assigned to the USS *Skipjack*.

A submarine crew is the ultimate team. Every person brings individual skills that enable a submarine to accomplish its warfare mission safely. You rely on each other to stay alive, which is a big incentive for good team play. Life aboard a submarine is disciplined but more relaxed than surface warships. If you serve on a sub, you claim there are two types of ships—submarines and targets. At sea, the day is eighteen hours long with six hours of a watch, six hours of work, and six hours of personal time, which includes time for sleep. The most responsibility in my life was underway as the Officer of the Deck, which means you oversee the sub's operations, and all other watch stations report to you. The most pressure I have experienced is directing the submarine to periscope depth in the Caribbean during the night. The periscope breaches the water, and suddenly you see the bright lights of a cruise ship. You have seconds to determine if you are in harm's way and immediately dive. Did I mention the bright lights? It is nearly impossible to see a cruise ship's green or red running lights with all the white lights. Going to periscope depth was a lot more pressure than I experienced taking the Maryland and Pennsylvania bar examinations or other stressful events in my life.

You do not read about too many mishaps with our fleet of submarines. Constant drills and practice range from a sudden nuclear reactor shutdown to warfare exercises to keep the crew sharp. These drills are realistic and remind the crew how much we depend on each other. Reactor safety is a priority, with regular scheduling of an Operational Reactor Safeguard Examination (ORSE). An ORSE includes a compliance audit, written exams, and intense simulation drills. I was the Engineering Officer of the Watch for an ORSE, which is stressful. I was lucky to join the *Skipjack* in the Mediterranean and had deployments to the North Atlantic and a goodwill UNITAS cruise to South American countries.

The *Skipjack* had an unfortunate incident when we participated in Caribbean naval exercises. We hit the ground, something you never want to do in a submarine. The Caribbean is challenging because the depth of water varies substantially. I was not on watch and was standing behind the conn (the control room) when suddenly the boat was violently shaking, accompanied by a thunderous scraping noise. The Officer of the Deck ordered an emergency surface. We had done emergency surfacing in drills, so this action was not different than what I experienced. I had no idea what had happened until the quartermaster announced we had hit the bottom of the ocean.

Five crew members flew to Groton, Connecticut, from Barbados for Admiral's mast, inquiring into the grounding facts and punishment if appropriate. The Commanding Officer (CO) arrived at his hearing and took full responsibility for the grounding since the CO signs off on all navigation charts, including the submarine's planned depth. The chart notes the ocean's depth. The CO was a leader, and I was disappointed with his departure because he was the best submarine warfare officer I had met. By chance and luck, I was the photography officer on the *Skipjack*. I was positioned on one of the two periscopes to take photographs while submerged. During a warfare exercise, the CO had me take photos of the surface ship's keel participating in the training. He autographed the pictures and presented them at the exercise wrap-up. I think it was lack of sleep during exercises that caused the CO's oversight with the navigation charts.

The Navigator also took full responsibility for the grounding but received no punishment. The Executive Officer (XO), the second in command of the ship, requested to testify at the hearing and advised the Admiral that he was responsible for the Navigator's mistake. The XO did not make sure the Navigator had enough sleep during the exercises. The XO received a letter of reprimand in his personnel file. The XO and the Navigator were leaders. You can see a trend here. The top three officers on the ship held themselves accountable for this accident.

The Officer of the Deck testified to the Admiral that he was too busy to keep track of the water's depth and was promptly discharged from the Navy. He was a nice guy but keeping track of the water's depth is critical in operating a submarine. The quartermaster is an enlisted crew member in charge of watch-to-watch navigation and the nautical charts' maintenance. The quartermaster testified in Admiral's mast that he saw the water's depth was decreasing and the submarine would hit the ground, but he did not feel it was his place to advise the Officer of the Deck. The Admiral discharged the quartermaster from the Navy. The Officer of the Deck and the Quartermaster Officer were not leaders, lacked accountability, and, even worse, not good team members. The grounding was the only serious accident I experienced in forty-two months, and I still remember being a member of a great team aboard the USS *Skipjack*.

Company Culture

Your company and its culture are a significant factor in the successful launch of a new product.

If I started a new company, I would copy Bill and Vieve Gore and organize it like they did when creating W.L. Gore & Associates. A caveat: It has been years since I worked for Gore, and my comments reflect my experiences, not necessarily the current company. Gore is a great company, and I was lucky to work there for more than twenty-two years. Bill Gore was in his late forties when he left a successful job at the DuPont Company to start Gore. According to their website, today it is a multinational manufacturing company specializing in medical, fabrics, industrial, and electrical products mainly derived from fluoropolymers with $3.8B in annual revenue and more than 11,000 Associates.

The Gore company is different and unique. It takes months for a new employee to understand the culture and maximize personal potential. My favorite element of the Gore culture is the lattice system. It is simple. You are free to reach out to anyone in the company to get your job done, and direct contact is encouraged. There is no need to ask your manager to speak to a leader, and there is no protocol for reaching out. Communication is not a free-for-all, and you have a personal responsibility not to waste people's time. An authoritarian structure can crush creativity, and the lattice system is the alternative.

Gore does not have titles, and all employees are Associates. I was fortunate to know Bill Gore before his death in 1986 and received some forceful coaching. I was one of five people in a polymer startup, and Bill and Vieve Gore would visit our startup on Wednesdays if in town, typically one to two times a month. Bill commented more than once that he enjoyed seeing the startup because it reminded him of the Gore company startup.

On a Wednesday, Bill arrived at our plant without Vieve while I met with the two other leaders in our small venture. We had a problem with an Associate who managed shipping, receiving, and facility maintenance. Multiple pallets containing toilet paper arrived at our shipping dock earlier that day, enough to last many years. I asked what was going on and learned he received a free barbecue grill if he ordered a high dollar value of supplies from a local vendor.

What do you do?

We had been discussing our options when Bill arrived and joined our meeting. Bill listened to our story and was visibly upset. He only asked one question. "How long have the three of you been discussing this problem?" I responded, "For forty-five minutes." Bill advised us to engage with Human Resources and fire the person. He explained that the individual was not a Gore Associate; he behaved as an employee. An Associate would never spend company money for personal benefit. He then sternly directed the three of us to get back to real work. So, you could be an employee of Gore, but not for long.

Gore has a charter that everyone could remember. "Make money and have fun." During my time at Gore, there were numerous attempts to update this charter. Most proposals were lots of big words that no one could remember. The first two words, "Make money," focus on a corporation's purpose and survival. "Have fun" has a broad meaning, but I always thought it referred to a positive work environment. For me, a positive workplace includes working for an ethical company with a commitment to product excellence and the environment.

Bill Gore articulated four cultural principles: freedom, fairness, commitment, and waterline. Like the charter, the beauty of these principles is they are easy to remember. I benefited from the freedom principle throughout my career as an engineer, a plant manager, and in general management and corporate development with Gore. Associates have the freedom to encourage, help, and allow other associates to grow in knowledge, skill, and scope of responsibility. The second principle is fairness, and I think this is aspirational. The concept of fairness is personal, and what is fair to one person may not be acceptable to another. The goal was to try to be fair, and it is not going to be perfect. Commitment is a straightforward principle. You make your commitments, and you keep them. Waterline is the final principle, and it requires Associates to consult with the appropriate people if the action could negatively impact Gore's reputation or profitability.

The Gore principles are the essential requirements of a good team. Freedom to make your commitments, try to be fair to people, and consult with others before taking risks.

Some new Associates fail at Gore for one reason—you must be a self-starter and proactive. Some manufacturing and quality jobs are subject to controls and training. Mainly, a team welcomes new people, offers a grounding, and expects you to engage and deliver value. Ask questions, seek opportunities to make an impact, make a few mistakes, and learn. Self-starters succeed and love the Gore company. My career at Gore is a bit unusual. In my interview with Gore, I explained that I was leaving DuPont because I wanted to broaden my responsibilities beyond engineering. I was curious about marketing and planned to go to graduate school to expand my education in the next five years. An interviewer asked me what I did not want to do at Gore, and I responded, "manufacturing leadership." At five years in Gore, I worked as a manufacturing leader. There was a need, I was able to fill it, and I loved being a plant manager.

The Gore website, gore.com, lists dozens of books and articles about the company, and it is an impressive summary. I love the Gore company. To be balanced, I will end my discussion of the Gore company with three observations that disappointed me. First, the Gore culture is like a religion to some Associates. To suggest it is not perfect was considered heresy by some leaders. The reality is Gore is a great company, but not perfect, as some people like to claim. Second, some of the Associates I worked for operated as if everything was waterline. I mentioned earlier that most managers are not leaders. Gore often hired intelligent people from other companies for leadership roles who memorized the Gore principles and objectives but did not embrace the intent. There were pockets of the company that operated like a sizable autocratic company rather than Gore. Third, Gore established several new products and business development teams. I was surprised that these teams' appointed leaders did not have success stories in product development. These Associates were managers who liked establishing a process for others to follow and somehow believed you could write a process and guarantee success in new products. Process and checklists are just helpful tools. No company can be perfect.

Overcoming Internal Obstacles

If you work for a company, then you will have to learn how to overcome internal obstacles. The number of barriers will be lower if you are lucky enough to work for an inspirational leader. You can hope your boss is an inspirational leader, but you will not likely be this lucky. I was aware that Ritchie Snyder "had my back" during my successful product launches without making it a big deal. I had a lot of freedom to make things happen quickly because of Ritchie, but I earned this freedom by keeping him informed. No surprises. Be happy if your boss is an outstanding manager. You can live with working for a good manager. Good luck if you have a lousy boss.

I keep a relatively low profile once my strategy and tactics survive a business review. I scheduled reviews every six months. One slide in these reviews listed planned actions for the next six months. If there were no objections, then I assumed I had the approval to act. Take yes for an answer.

Be transparent, especially with bad news. Effectively communicating mistakes and a corrective action plan builds trust, and leadership will allow you to make mistakes and learn from them.

Always be persistent. I never heard "No" from my leadership when I made a pitch for an investment or planned tactic. Instead, I heard, "Not now." So, I would try again and again, acknowledging concerns from past discussions. I can be annoying.

The following combines two tactics in overcoming internal obstacles. I forum shop at times. I needed permission to hire a Gore IT Associate to develop a customer relationship software for ELIXIR Strings on weekends, with additional pay. The investment was small, but I knew our IT department would disapprove of the project. I went to one of Gore's best attorneys and received guidance on engaging the Associate legally for weekend work. I advised Human Resources of the legal advice, and they went along with my plan. The next part of the lesson is dangerous and should not be a frequent event. Seek forgiveness, not permission. IT leadership was quite upset when he found out about the successful software tool. Everyone survived, and I had an essential tool. I promised I would not engage IT resources for weekend projects in the future.

I was not able to launch several new products in Gore. In hindsight, my product story needed to be more compelling for several of these products. More details might have made the difference, or maybe not? Today, I would spend more time building a strategic plan for these new ideas so that leadership had a complete story.

1-2-3

I offer some final advice when presenting to leaders and managers. These are busy people who do not want to know everything you know. So, take care to figure out what they need to know to help you succeed.

I suggest the following protocol when meeting with leaders and managers: 1-2-3.

1. Use crisp communication of valuable information. Limit any answers to questions to thirty seconds when possible. Excellent responses include "yes, no, I do not know, but I will get back to you."

2. If in-person, make good eye contact. Do not stare wildly, but lack of eye contact suggests you are not comfortable or uncertain.

3. Use an even tone of voice, and end sentences with confidence, not a questioning tone.

That is it, and practice communicating with leaders makes perfect.

Lesson 5. Leadership and Team Lessons

- Do your best to be an inspirational leader. Attributes include smart, strategic, good judgment, accountable, learner, honest, loyal, and respectful.

- If your boss is not a leader, hope they are a good manager. You can live with this.

- Leaders create an innovative environment and take joy in helping team members grow and succeed.

- Build a great team by hiring people who are more intelligent than you and have needed skill sets.

- W.L. Gore & Associates ("Gore") is a great company started by Bill and Vieve Gore in 1958. Like Gore, build a culture on your team of excellent communication and practice principles like fairness, freedom, commitment, and waterline. May you be lucky enough to work for a company like Gore.

- If someone tells you "no," hear "not now." Forum shop and seek forgiveness only if an activity critical for success is likely to be disapproved by bureaucracy.

- Communications with leaders and busy managers should be crisp, make eye contact, and use an even tone of voice.

Lesson 6. The Important Numbers

Finance for Non-Finance People

Thank goodness for spreadsheets. This lesson offers an easy lesson in building your first income statement and identifies the necessary guardrails to keep you on the road to business success. Finance professionals are concerned with hundreds of financial metrics. My advice is for the launch team to focus on a few critical financial objectives and keep them simple. Then, consult regularly with finance professionals for the hard stuff.[4]

Revenue Forecast

Your financial plan begins with a revenue forecast. Understanding revenue opportunities early in a project is crucial to ensure the view will be worth the climb.

Revenue is your value price times the number of units sold, an easy calculation. Lesson 3 detailed pricing, and this is one-half of your projected revenue calculation. If you thought pricing was complex, now try to predict the annual number of units you will sell for the first five years. I have bad news. You will be wrong with whatever number of units you predict for

---

[4] I was lucky to work with Shanti Mehta, who was the Chief Financial Officer for W.L. Gore & Associates for most of the time I was with the company. Shanti is a brilliant finance leader, and he enjoys teaching. Shanti released multiple memorandums coaching employees on finance terms, and a set of forms for annual business planning. Shanti's written materials and personal coaching enabled me to embrace essential data that helped me build successful businesses.

your first business plan. But you must start the process so that you can continually improve the prediction.

My sales forecast for GLIDE Floss was ridiculously low but met expectations. Unfortunately, ELIXIR Strings sales forecast was overly optimistic, and it took about one year longer for sales to match my revenue prediction. This was a painful year. For ELIXIR Strings, I made assumptions on the number of independent music stores that decided to purchase the product by month, and I assumed I would match unit sales of the leading guitar string SKU. I was too optimistic about how much time it would take for music retailers to stock the product.

GLIDE Floss and ELIXIR Strings' first revenue forecast is an educated guess. As you learn, regularly update the forecast. Fortunately, there is a ton of market data available to begin your analysis. I will use GLIDE Floss as an example. I had access to sales of the top-selling dental floss SKU in drugstores. My first revenue projection assumed sales in drugstores only since they were more receptive to offering new and multiple dental floss product options to their customers. My sales goal in five years was to match the revenue, not units, of the leading SKU. The wholesale price of GLIDE Floss was much higher than the leading SKU, so my unit forecast was about 1/3 of the unit sales of the leading SKU. I was too conservative in my first forecast, and I was fortunate that leadership approving the project understood my first guess was low. My drugstore dental floss market share forecast was about 3%. An exceptionally low forecast will raise havoc on manufacturing capacity and planning. GLIDE Floss production struggled to keep up with demand for the first two years following launch. My low unit forecast was the driver for insufficient manufacturing capacity investments. Who would have guessed that GLIDE Floss would be the #1 (mint) and # 3 (unflavored) selling SKUs in retail within sixteen months of launch? I did not guess this.

Expense Definitions

Lesson 3 includes the following diagram of price and costs, and I have circled the types of expenses that must become your best friends in Figure 6.1.

Figure 6.1 Expenses

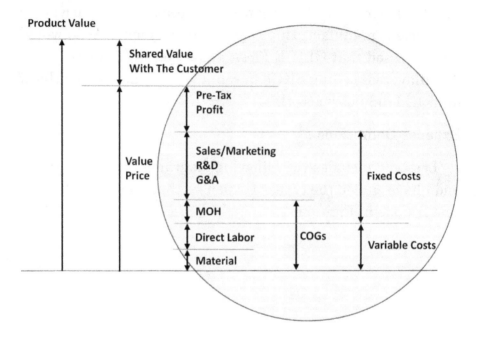

Here we go:

There are two types of costs: (1) Variable Costs and (2) Fixed Costs.

Variable Costs = Materials + Direct Labor

As the name suggests, variable costs vary with the number of products produced and sold to a customer. The following are accepted definitions of materials and direct labor:

- Materials. All raw material costs, cost of outside processing, packaging materials, and product labels.

- Direct Labor. Direct labor is all labor directly engaged in production, including inspection, quality control, and packaging.

Fixed Costs = Manufacturing Overhead (MOH) + Selling Expenses (SOH) + Research and Development (R&D) + General & Administrative (G&A)

Fixed costs are also called period costs, and the four buckets of expenses noted above do not change as the production goes up or down.

> *Note. Direct labor is sometimes included as a fixed cost if the company does not have the ability or systems to cut back on manufacturing employee hours when production slows.*

The following are definitions of the four fixed costs.

- Manufacturing Overhead (MOH). These are the indirect costs supporting manufacturing a product. For example, think of expenses like the machine shop, production planning, production leadership, manufacturing equipment depreciation, utility costs, and manufacturing supplies.

- Selling Expenses (SOH). SOH is the salaries and expenses of all employees in selling and marketing, marketing costs like advertisements, samples, sales meetings, and other related selling costs.

- Research & Development (R&D). All expenses associated with scientists, engineers, and technicians developing new products or improving existing products. R&D includes costs like salaries, benefits, consulting, professional dues, and subscriptions.

- General & Administrative (G&A). G&A is the final bucket and includes all remaining expenses not included in MOH, SOH, and R&D. Typically, this consists of human resources, the finance department, and the legal department.

We are almost done. The final numbers in the income statement are:

- Cost of Goods Sold (COGs) = Materials + Direct Labor + MOH

- Gross Margin, % = (Revenue – COGs) / Revenue

COGs are all expenses related to manufacturing your product and delivering it to your customer. COGs analysis was essential in GLIDE Floss and ELIXIR Strings, where we sampled lots of products. The costs of the samples are COGs, and this is a marketing expense in sampling programs.

Finally:

- Pre-Tax Profit = Revenue – (Variables Costs + Fixed Costs)

You now have all the information to assemble a simple income statement for your new product launch, and it is easy to format this into a simple spreadsheet.

Figure 6.2. Simple Income Statement Format

Income Statement	Year 1	Year 2	Year 3	Year 4	Year 5
Revenue					
Material					
Direct Labor					
Variable Costs					
Mfg Overheads (MOH)					
Cost of Goods Sold (COGs)					
Gross Margin, %					
Selling Costs (SOH)					
Research & Development (R&D)					
General & Administrative (G&A)					
Pre-Tax Profits					
Pre-Tax Profits, %					

Financial Guardrails

Guardrails are popular in business and provide guidance to ensure a financial plan's alignment with business objectives. Unfortunately, financial guardrail guidance will vary depending on the product and the market, so no one-size-fits-all.

The following are my preferred guardrails for branded consumer products like GLIDE Floss and ELIXIR Strings. But, of course, your financial guardrails might be higher or lower depending on the product.

- Revenue. Minimum five-year likely forecast of $5M, with an opportunity to grow to greater than $20M.

  o This total can be from the sale of multiple SKUs. Revenue less than $5M will make it challenging to cover likely costs in marketing and sales and deliver a preferred pre-tax profit. Also, who wants to work hard to build a business of less than $5M in retail sales? Years ago, I enjoyed asking MBAs what is preferable, a $100M business with one product line or a company with $100M in sales from twenty products, each with $5M in annual sales? Most MBAs preferred the $100M business with one product to have the scale to make investments with improved focus. However, I like the idea of twenty products. It is like placing twenty different bets.

- Pre-Tax Profit. Target 30% in the five-year forecast.

  o 30% is an excellent profit margin, and it is always my goal for a new business. Remember, a company's purpose is to earn a profit distributed to investors or reinvested in the company. My first income statement attempts to achieve a 30% pre-tax profit in Year 5. Striving for a 30% projected margin means you will likely be above 20%, which is my minimum pre-tax profit guardrail. I wish I had a dime for every person who has warned me that sales are typically predicted high, and expenses typically predicted low. Experienced businesspeople will be skeptical of sales and costs for all the right reasons.

- Maximum 40% Gross Margin.

  o If COGs are more than 40%, then it might be challenging to meet pre-tax profit expectations for a consumer product.

- I prefer to have up to 30% of revenue available for SOH for a consumer product. Note that SOH will typically be lower, and COGs will be higher for a component product or a finished product sold in an industrial market.

- Plan to invest 4% of revenue to fund R&D. This is only $400,000 for a $10M business, which is not a lot of money.

- Assume G&A requires 5% of your revenue.

A few words of advice:

- You decide the price of your product. Share the product's value with your customer, but do not price your product low with the hope that people will more likely accept your offering. Consumers will buy your product if it is worth it.

- Lowering costs is difficult and might compromise your product launch. For example, lowering SOH to improve pre-tax profits by reducing GLIDE Floss or ELIXIR Strings samples might have destroyed the grassroots marketing strategy.

- Consider outsourcing manufacturing steps that are not proprietary to reduce direct labor and MOH. Only outsource to companies that focus on operational excellence, and they might be a better option than developing more expensive capability in-house. Never outsource proprietary manufacturing processes. For example, I outsourced selected manufacturing steps in GLIDE Floss and ELIXIR Strings, but Gore accomplished proprietary fiber manufacturing and coating of guitar strings.

- Projections of ELIXIR Strings direct labor costs made manufacturing automation a requirement. Pre-tax profit expectations would not be achieved without automation.

Your First Forecast Income Statement

In the first ninety days, create and review a simple five-year income statement. Assembling your first income statement can be overwhelming when you have more questions than answers. But building an income statement early in the project will substantially improve your focus.

I only estimate six numbers when creating my first income statement. The income statement will be wrong, but I now have a path to improving uncertainty. Estimate the following numbers.

- Year 1, 2, and 3 revenues equal your value price times the annual forecasted units.

- Year 3 material.

- Year 3 direct labor.

- Year 3 MOH.

A piece of cake. Now, use the following assumptions listed in Figure 6.3 to create your first income statement.

Figure 6.3. Assumptions for Your First Income Statement

Income Statement	Year 1	Year 2	Year 3	Year 4	Year 5
Revenue	Estimate = Price x Units	Estimate = Price x Units	Estimate = Price x Units	= Year 3 x 10%	= Year 4 x 10%
Material	Assume Year 3 % = 25%	Assume Year 3 % = 25%	Estimate Year 3 w/ First BOM	Assume Same % as Year 3	Assume Same % as Year 3
Direct Labor	Assume Year 3 % = 50%	Assume Year 3 % = 50%	Estimate Year 3	Assume Same % as Year 3	Assume Same % as Year 3
Variable Costs	Calculate	Calculate	= Material + Direct Labor	Calculate	Calculate
Mfg Overheads (MOH)	Assume Year 3 % = 50%	Assume Year 3 % = 50%	Estimate Year 3	Assume Same % as Year 3	Assume Same % as Year 3
Cost of Goods Sold (COGs)	Calculate	Calculate	= Variable Costs + MOH	Calculate	Calculate
Gross Margin, %	Calculate	Calculate	= 1 - COGs / Revenue	Calculate	Calculate
Selling Costs (SOH)	Assume Same $ as Year 3	Assume Same $ as Year 3	25% to 30% of Year 3 Revenue	Assume 30% of Revenue	Assume 30% of Revenue
Research & Development (R&D)	Assume Same $ as Year 3	Assume Same $ as Year 3	4% of Year 3 Revenue	Assume 4% of Revenue	Assume 4% of Revenue
General & Administrative (G&A)	Assume Same $ as Year 3	Assume Same $ as Year 3	5% of Year 3 Revenue	Assume 5% of Revenue	Assume 5% of Revenue
Pre-Tax Profits	Calculate	Calculate	= (1 - COGSs) - (SOH + R&D + G&A)	Calculate	Calculate
Pre-Tax Profits, %	Calculate	Calculate	= Pre-Tax Profits / Revenue	Calculate	Calculate

Figure 6.4 below is an example of your first income statement with the following assumptions.

- Estimated Year 1 revenue $1M, Year 2 revenue $4M, Year 3 revenue $10M.

- Estimated Year 3 material is 22% of revenue.

- Estimated Year 3 direct labor is 3% of revenue.

- Year 3 MOH is 10% of revenue.

Figure 6.4. Your First Income Statement - Example

Income Statement, M$	Year 1	Year 2	Year 3	Year 4	Year 5
Revenue	1.00	4.00	10.00	11.00	12.10
Material	0.28	1.10	2.20	2.42	2.66
Direct Labor	0.05	0.18	0.30	0.33	0.36
Variable Costs	0.32	1.28	2.50	2.75	3.03
Mfg Overheads (MOH)	0.15	0.40	1.00	1.10	1.21
Cost of Goods Sold (COGs)	0.47	1.68	3.50	3.85	4.24
Gross Margin, %	53%	58%	65%	65%	65%
Selling Costs (SOH)	3.00	3.00	3.00	3.30	3.63
Research & Development (R&D)	0.40	0.40	0.40	0.44	0.48
General & Administrative (G&A)	0.50	0.50	0.50	0.55	0.61
Pre-Tax Profits	-3.37	-1.58	2.60	2.86	3.15
Pre-Tax Profits, %	-337%	-40%	26%	26%	26%

As previously mentioned, your first income statement is wrong, and this is okay. You have been working on the project for less than ninety days, and you will correct errors as you learn. Immediately prioritize uncertainty and focus on improving the most in doubt estimates (e.g., guesses).

The following are observations from the Figure 6.4 example.

- I like the potential for this project to make money. First estimates satisfy minimum financial guardrails in Year 3.

- Revenue growth from Year 2 to Year 3 feels optimistic. I would compare $10M Year 3 estimated revenue to market share. If market share is relatively low and your grassroots marketing plan is effective, this might be reasonable.

- This project does not break even until Year 4 due to relatively high negative pre-tax profits in Year 1 and Year 2. Key drivers to evaluate are revenue estimates and high SOH investments. Do not underestimate Year 1 and Year 2 SOH required for success, but a bottoms-up SOH forecast may allow you to sharpen your pencil and improve the time for the project to break even.

- Figure. 6.4 in spreadsheet format allows you to perform basic sensitivity analysis. For example, what if direct labor and MOH are twice your first estimate? High direct labor or MOH might force an early discussion on automation or outsourcing.

- Your first income statement is a source to identify critical project issues for your business plan.

Congratulations. You now have your first five-year forecasted income statement, and updates must be made as you continue to learn.

The Basics – Free Cash Flow

Business is complicated, and you must be sure that you have enough cash on hand when you need it. You will be buying material to manufacture the product and owe your suppliers money based on accepted payment terms. You will sell the product to your customer, but you will receive the money owed based on accepted receivable terms. The joke is that you can make a lot of money and go broke because you have no cash. A business trend is for customers to extend their payment terms significantly, and 120-days is not unusual.

Ouch. You are financing your customer for four months, maybe more.

Cash Flow =

(1) Net After-Tax Profit plus Depreciation/Amortization

(2) Minus Increase in Receivables

(3) Minus Increase in Inventories

(4) Minus Decrease in Payables

(5) Minus Decrease in Debt

(6) Minus Increase in Fixed Capital Investment at Cost

A few definitions:

- Depreciation is the reduction in the value of a business asset over time.

- Amortization is like depreciation but reduces an intangible asset's value, like a patent, over time.

- Receivables are the amount of money owed by customers for purchases made with credit terms. You will typically want payment for your product in thirty days from shipment. Good luck. Larger companies are extending their payable terms to as many as 120 days.

- Payables are the amount of money you owe suppliers for purchases made with credit terms. Typical payment terms for small businesses are thirty days from the date of invoice or shipment.

You can positively influence cash flow by increasing net after-tax profits, including raising your price or lowering costs. You can insist on receiving money due in a short time, and on the other hand, slow your payment to suppliers to improve payables. I suggest you not spend time playing games with receivable and payable terms. Stay with industry standards and enforce them.

Inventory is always a hot topic, and there is a golden rule for you to remember—all inventory is bad unless it is good.

Clear as mud. The three buckets of inventory are (1) Raw Materials (RM), (2) Work-in-Process (WIP), and (3) Finished Goods (FG).

Definitions:

- Raw Materials (RM). The exact definition as Materials in the Income Statement; all raw material costs, outside processing, packaging materials, and product labels.

- Work-in-Process (WIP). WIP can be complicated because it is the value of the product at various stages of completion. If manufacturing is short and straightforward, WIP may be extremely low. However, if complicated, multiple steps might take weeks of processing, then WIP could be huge.

- Finished Goods (FG). Products that are packaged and ready for shipping to customers.

Minimize all inventories. Early in the project, you might be tempted to purchase 100,000 blister cards for just 20% more than 10,000 blister cards with the volume discount. In the beginning, order the number of blister cards you need. It is a good bet your packaging will require updates sooner than later, and you do not want to be sitting on 90,000 obsolete blister cards that you paid an extra 20%.

I was challenged by the negative impact of FG inventory early in GLIDE Floss. For the first year of the project, I kept more than $100,000 of FG inventory, sitting in warehouse racks and waiting for shipment to the latest customer. Large retailers demand immediate delivery of products when they finally decide to purchase. You must maintain inventory to cover the expected large stocking orders for these customers. If not, you will lose the order. I considered this finished goods inventory to be "good" inventory. Remember, all inventory is bad unless it is good.

I toured our contract manufacturing packaging plant for GLIDE Floss with Gore leadership before being fired from the project. They were checking out the FG inventory in the warehouse adjacent to shipping docks. Leadership consensus was I needed to learn how to manage FG inventory. Have you ever seen more than a million dollars of packaged dental floss that will ship to customers in the next two to three days? It is a lot of boxes and looks overwhelming. I do not believe my explanation was well-received. But, the reality is we were effectively managing inventory.

The bottom line is to make inventory management a priority and differentiate between good inventory and bad inventory.

I have a reminder from Lesson 3 and pricing. What do you do when a customer extends payment terms to 120 days from thirty days? This customer is strategic, and the customer will not take no for an answer. The answer is easy. Accept the 120-day terms and work with an accountant to raise your price to more than cover the cost of the additional 90-day payment terms.

The Impact of Lowering Product Price

In Lesson 3, I mentioned the ELIXIR Strings business leadership changed the pricing strategy and discounted electric strings MSRP from $15 per set to $12 per set, a 20% price decrease after my departure. A new logo and packaging accompanied the price decrease. Of course, the claim was electric string sales increased 10% with a new logo and packaging. My bet is the 10% increase in unit sales had more to do with the price decrease, but I do not know.

(1) What is the impact of lowering the price by 20% on the business, with no increase in unit sales?

Answer: Pre-tax profit decreases 11%. You work the same, and you make less money. I do not claim to be the smartest guy in the room, but this makes no sense.

(2) What is the impact of lowering the price by 20% on the business, with a 10% increase in unit sales?

Answer: Pre-tax profit decreases 6%. You work harder, and you make less money. Like question (1) above, this makes no sense to me.

(3) How much do unit sales need to increase with a price decrease of 20% to make the same pre-tax profit?

Answer: 25% increase in unit sales, a significant percentage.

I do not know ELIXIR Strings margins, so I made up my numbers and percentages to match my earlier guardrail margin guidance. Before lowing the price by 20%, I assumed sales of 1,000,000 units, $7.50 wholesale unit price, 25% variable costs, 45% fixed costs, and 30% pre-tax profits.

The lesson is decreasing the product's price may increase unit sales but will likely reduce your profits. Work smart, not hard. Think twice about lowering your price.

Lesson 6. Important Numbers Lessons

- You do not have to be an accountant or a financial wizard to launch a new product but take the time to learn the basics and work closely with finance experts on the hard stuff.

- You will likely overestimate revenue and underestimate your costs in developing your first forecasted five-year income statement. Do your best to be objective and not overly conservative or too optimistic.

- Create your first five-year income statement forecast within ninety days of initiating the project. Creating an income statement will drive healthy discussions about value pricing, unit sales, and managing costs. Do not worry. Your first income statement will be wrong, but it is always easier to edit than create. Prioritize on the factors that have the most impact on your profitability.

- Establish financial guardrails to avoid alignment issues with pricing and costs. Critical metrics include minimum revenue expectations for a new product. I prefer $5M minimum likely sales and maximum variable and fixed costs of 70% of sales; maximum 70% costs mean a pre-tax profit of 30%.

- Cash flow analysis is essential. Focus on improving cash flow by increasing revenue, lowering costs, lowering receivables, increasing payables, and reducing inventories. Of course, you can influence these cash flow variables in your day-to-day operations. But do not play games with absurd receivable and payable terms.

- All inventory is bad unless it is good. Therefore, minimize all inventories and proactively decide when inventories are required.

- Beware—lowering the price of your product will typically result in you working harder for less money.

Ruminations

Perhaps the most crucial lesson of Successful Grassroots Product Launches is how much fun you will have. You will meet all sorts of characters in the marketplace, and better yet, have the opportunity to build a team. If the product is successful, then people have jobs. Hopefully, satisfying jobs if you are an inspirational leader.

My working title for this book was *Passion – Focus – Urgency*. You need these traits to be successful in launching a new product. I gave up on this title as I wrote the lessons from the GLIDE Floss and ELIXIR Strings stories. It occurred to me that you cannot teach either passion or urgency. You either have these traits, or you do not. My experience is people who gravitate to new ideas and product launches are passionate and impatient. You can teach a person to be more focused. But do not let a manager claim you need to focus to avoid the risk of a product launch.

I mentioned the term "best practice" in many of the lessons. The definition of a best practice is the way I like to do it. You will develop many best practices as you launch a new product. Take care not to be a slave to your success. I have mentioned several times that I am never more creative than when I do not know what I am doing. Always keep an open mind. Most important, strive to be an inspirational leader.

There are hundreds of people that made GLIDE Floss and ELIXIR Strings successful. I am thankful to my wife, Pamela, for her continued support in my crazy career. Product launches are stressful on you but might even be more stressful at times for your family. Thank you, Pam.

Just remember.

Innovate—Disrupt—Make Money—Have Fun.

That is all, folks. I wish you the best of success in launching your new product, and I hope the stories and lessons in this book have been helpful.

John S.

Bucktown Grand Slam

John@bucktowngrandslam.com

Index